# EARLE

12-31-00

Pat:

A great Buckeye fan.

Go Bucks!

Earle Bruce

# EARLE

## A Coach's Life

by EARLE BRUCE

with George and Darcy Lehner

ORANGE FRAZER *PRESS*
*Wilmington, Ohio USA*
*2000*

ISBN 1-882203-62-3

Additional copies of *Earle: A Coach's Life* or other Orange Frazer Press publications may be ordered directly from:

Orange Frazer Press, Inc.
Box 214
37 ½ West Main Street
Wilmington, Ohio 45177

Telephone 1.800.852.9332 for price and shipping information
Web Site: www.orangefrazer.com

Jacket design by Tim Fauley
Cover photograph, and ones on pages 44, 49, 54, 74, 104, 108, 113, 119, 125, 135, 146, 154, 161, 166 by Chance Brockway; others from collections of Michele Bruce and the coach

Library of Congress Cataloging-in-Publication Data

Bruce, Earle, 1931-
    Earle, a coach's life / by Earle Bruce as told to George and Darcy Lehner.
       p. cm.
    Includes index.
    ISBN 1-882203-62-3 (alk. paper)
    1. Bruce, Earle, 1931- 2. Football coaches--United States--Biography.  I. Title: Earle.
    II. Lehner, George, 1951- III. Lehner, Darcy, 1958- IV. Title.

GV939.B783 A3 2000
796.332'63'092-dc21
    [B]

                                                    00-055740

This book is dedicated to my wife of 45 years, Jean, who raised our four daughters almost singlehandedly, with only a small helping hand from me; to my four daughters, Lynn, Michele, Aimee, and Noel, who at one time or another ran the household; to all the assistant coaches too numerous to name, and the secretaries, trainers, and equipment men who helped make coaching such a great experience for me; and to the game of football, which I have always loved.

# Acknowledgements

In theory, writing a book should be a straightforward task. In practice, it is not. This experience has left us grateful to many people along the way.

—To Perry and Ellen for always believing; all the Bruce women for sharing their memories and time—especially Jean and Michele. Your kindness and graciousness is boundless; friends, colleagues and former players who remembered stories about Earle's stories; Chance Brockway for generous access to his photo files; John Baskin and Marcy Hawley, immense gratitude for not only their considerable professional gifts but also their fortitude, tenacity, and comedic relief.

—Appreciation to our friends who tolerated our preoccupation and helped manage our daily chaos: Libby, Carole, Louie, Beth, Joan, and Angela, your encouragement and generosity makes everything possible; gratitude to Karen, my cherished roommate and confidante; Pat, the consummate friend, lifelong safety net, and saving grace; thanks to Mom and Tabby for your love and enthusiasm; to Rob, DeeDee, and Shannon, for your patience and support during my countless computer hours. You are my life's most precious commodity; to Alice and Frank Lehner, whose pride emanates from above; to RGL, your zest for life and love is priceless.

—And in memory of my father, Robert K. Strang (1926–1990), whose shining example of character, selflessness, and unconditional love never dims with time.

*—DL, June, 2000*

# Contents

# Foreword

Extracting the story of Earle Bruce is somewhat like a dental procedure. The removal of any bothersome tooth is a delicate yet necessary
exercise. As any reasonable dental practitioner would justify, it had to
come out, and so did the true tale of Earle.

For almost two years we've extracted this story in a painstaking
manner, enlisting the help of Earle's family, friends, former players, and
colleagues. The most formidable challenge of chronicling Earle's football
life, is the nature of the man himself. Throughout his career, Earle
blocked out much of life's static to devote himself to coaching. That
powerful focus was both strength and flaw, because it served as a blinder
to the ever fickle local climate.

While Earle preoccupied himself with being a winning coach, the
campus politics around him kept churning. Never an image-conscious
man, Earle was gradually forced to acknowledge the significance of this
nebulous concept. Image would prove a serendipitous and powerful force
in his coaching life. Earle's focus was so single-minded, writing his story
actually became much like laboring over a huge and complex jigsaw
puzzle. We started at the edge, and we pieced the events of his life together.

Earle relished the opportunity to be candid. We learned many of the
public notions about him were contrived and misconceived—mostly out
of context. For reasons of libel and slander, some of his stories will never

be printed. The pain of his Ohio State and Colorado State dismissals was still palpable in recalling those events. Earle's account of the forces behind his demise were fascinating, some of the details contemptible. His anecdotes with former players, and, of course, Woody Hayes, were a delight. He discussed coaching not only in the technical sense but also in the context of a time-honored profession.

Earle would be an oddity in the coaching world of today. He is incapable of pretentiousness, loves his family unabashedly, and thinks like a coach—not a businessman. He would still be unable to assume a politically correct demeanor. He scoffs at gender equity. The lines of right and wrong are still distinct to Earle. He has never developed the ability to be disingenuous.

Coaching is Earle's being—his DNA. Throughout the bumps in his journey, he remained true to the core of the profession. His coaching apprenticeship was comprised of hard knocks and harder work. His career reads like a case study in tenacity and self-motivation. He is a veteran recipient of many kicks in the teeth, and yet he exited the coaching ranks remarkably intact, carrying away an extraordinary won-loss record, professional integrity, and enough memories for several coaching lifetimes.

—Darcy and George Lehner
*Spring, 2000*

# EARLE

# On the Way

My hometown might have been a movie set for any film depicting small town America. The population of Cumberland, Maryland, numbered around 35,000 blue collar folks, six of whom were Bruce children. The age gap of my siblings made it feel almost like

*⊃A is for Applause: a young Earle Bruce is wooed by Maryland coach Jim Tatum*

there were two families in one. I was the second born with an older sister, Mary Lou, and a younger sister, Beverly. We were only about 18 months apart in age. Then nine years later, the next group of Bruces began to make an appearance. Three boys in a row—my brothers, Ronnie, Bobby, and Barry. It was quite an adjustment for all of us. I remember coming home from college when my brothers were little. I'd be home for a break and my little brother would go in my room and watch me sleep. Then he'd go to Mother and say, 'That man's here again. That man is here AGAIN.'

---

My Dad used to throw and catch with me from the time I could walk. When I played in the 'cradle league', he worked as the umpire. I was the pitcher and he was awfully tough on me. 'Put 'em over. Put 'em over,' he'd say. Dad was a great sandlot ball player. He played for the old Book Shoes semipro team in Pittsburgh, and he drove his old gravity flow

Model-T Ford backwards up the hills of Mt. Washington to make sure he didn't run out of gas.

When I was a kid, I always thought I would be a baseball player, too. The Book Shoes played teams like the Homestead Grays from the old black league, but it was the big time to me. I was the bat boy when I was about four, and the team gave me a baseball uniform. I loved the feeling of being part of something.

**I WAS IN LOVE WITH THE GAME OF BASEBALL,** until the curve ball hit me. My problem was—I couldn't hit *it*. When I was a junior in high school I batted .489, and I was fast. I went to some tryout camps, but when they threw the curve ball, I was in trouble. The curve ball ended my baseball career and propelled me to a new one—football.

Dad loved football and always came and watched me play. He'd get on me for not using my stiff-arm. He always admonished me. 'Don't let anyone get to you unless they first get an arm in their face,' he said. But my mother was the most vocal at any game. One time my high school team was playing at Johnstown, Pennsylvania. I took the kickoff and ran it 95 yards for the touchdown. She ran all 95 yards with me—down our sidelines. Sometimes, she embarrassed me a little bit. I'd try and get her to settle down but she wouldn't. It wasn't her nature.

WWII was going on and my high school, Allegheny, was a football power in the state of Maryland. Because of the war, coaches were a scarce commodity. My coach told me he wanted me to move to fullback. Coach Bowers was a good football coach, but his sport was really basketball. He was pulling double-duty as the football coach. Even though I weighed in at 135 pounds, I gave it a shot. When the real football coach, Bob Pence, came back from the service, he kept me at fullback, too. I scored 23 touchdowns my senior year, which was a record in western Maryland for some time.

I didn't really play a lot until I was a junior because as a sophomore I had broken my collarbone, and I sat out the whole year. But I could run. I already knew that. As a sophomore, I ran a 10-second hundred-yard dash on an old cinder track, with no starting blocks. Nobody used blocks. For a start, we just dug holes in the cinders and put our feet in the holes.

My junior year, I played fullback at 140 pounds between two big halfbacks who blocked for me. My play was the pitch-sweep, fullback around end. If the halfback got a block on the end, it was *bon voyage*, because of my speed. No one ever really defensed our pitch that year.

The halfbacks weren't quite as keen on this play as I was—all through practice, every day, they practiced blocking the linemen, and I went over by myself and practiced quick-kicks. The coach didn't want me getting hurt.

'We have *never* used a quick-kick,' the halfbacks pointed out to me, while I pointed out to them proper blocking techniques on the big defensive end.

We were terrible my junior year. Cumberland was west, not too far from Pittsburgh, sandwiched between Pennsylvania and West Virginia, and kids could drive over into West Virginia and buy beer at age 14. But ours was an unusual class; we were guys who had started out as sophomores together, and we had gotten really close. We liked Bob Pence—he was a young guy who lived on our street, and on his way home from school he might just walk in the house and ask how you were. We wanted to play for him, and we didn't want to disappoint him. So we decided to obey the rules.

**BY THE TIME *WE* WERE SENIORS,** we had an attitude. Those were some glory days. We ran the old Shaughnessy-T, which featured a man in motion in a T-formation and also a flanker T, and I called the plays as the fullback. One of our first scrimmages was against Romney Deaf and Dumb—that's what the school was called back then—and they had a helluva team. They used an 'over shifted 6' and we were running a flanker system, but they were overcommitting to it. I asked the coach why we couldn't run to the other side.

'We don't have a play to go over there,' he said.

21

◌ *Earle, center, prepares to block for his best friend, Wesley Abrams, with ball*

So we got the shit beat out of us. Afterwards at practice, Coach Pence was mad and declared, 'Earle, I want you to call the plays.'

So we put in the counter play to get the ball back to the weak side and I called the plays for the entire season. We went undefeated in nine games. The only blemish on our record was a 6-6 tie with our crosstown rival, Fort Hill, who was having a great season, too, and had exactly the same kind of kids we did. It was our big Thanksgiving game, and it wasn't the way we wanted to end the season. We scored first, so we said that we didn't tie them, *they* tied *us*. That's how we figured it.

In three years, I never lost a 220-yard dash, and I was beaten only once in the hundred. I was the state track champion in the 220. Track and baseball seasons ran at the same time and I was the only player in the school allowed to play both sports. I practiced track during the lunch hour and baseball after school. I was a rough scrappy kind of kid.

**I DID TRY TO PLAY SOME BASKETBALL**, mainly because of my lifelong friend, Wes Abrams. He had a deadly jump shot, but in my sophomore year, Coach Bowers cut Wes from the team and kept me. The coach said all Wes had going was that one shot. I was as devastated as Wes was. Basketball was everything to him. I just played the game because it let me pal around with Wes.

I played a pretty rough version of basketball, which Coach Bowers didn't appreciate much. I hit one of the star players once in practice. I had gotten decked and as the player was standing over me, I reached up and grabbed both his feet. He crashed to the floor, and, boy, did the coach get on my ass. Then he threw me off the court.

For the first junior varsity game, Coach Bowers told me to dress for the other team. Our opponents, the 7-7 Club, didn't bring enough players, so Coach threw me a green jersey and said he wanted me to play for them.

I thought he had left the room, so I slammed the jersey down and said, 'I'll be a sonofabitch. You wait three years to play and all of a sudden they put you on the other team.'

I did not neglect my vocabulary, but I did neglect my audience. As I was yelling and swearing, I turned around and saw Coach Bowers standing right behind me. Not my best move, but characteristic.

On the first play, they tipped the ball and I knocked two people over getting it and took it in for a basket. Those were the only points I scored. I was so worked up I played like a demon. After about five minutes, I decided that was enough. That was my last game.

COACH JIM TATUM, the University of Maryland football coach, came to Cumberland immediately after the 1949 season. He stayed at the Algonquin Hotel, one of the two hotels in town. His recruiting strategy was to invite players to his room from each of the three high schools in the area. As I walked into his room, I see Coach Tatum laying on the bed. He's about 6' 4" and his feet are hanging over the end of the bed.

His white dress shirt is unbuttoned, his tie undone and—he's smoking a cigarette. I don't like smoking, and, anyway, what is a coach doing smoking in front of kids who are told *not* to smoke? So here's this coach from the University of Maryland, trying to recruit me, and he's smoking.

Then he has twelve kids walk into his room and he asks everybody to give their name and weight as they parade past him lying there.

I knew at the moment that even if they really wanted me, I wasn't going to Maryland. I didn't know how the real world worked at that point in my life—but I knew this was a very unprofessional way to recruit somebody.

When he came to me, he asked how tall I was.

I said I was 5'9" and weighed 160 pounds.

He looked at me and said, sarcastically, 'Soakin' wet?'

I really only weighed 155.

I was eyeballing him and thinking, 'How interested could he really be, all these kids in here. Shouldn't he be talking to me by myself?' I was young and didn't know much, but I thought he didn't show much interest, and it wasn't how I pictured an interview going. I knew right then that I wasn't going to Maryland.

Then Maryland began recruiting me for track. They offered fifty per cent aid for track and the other fifty per cent aid for football. But it was too late. I had already made up my mind I wasn't going there.

A month or so later a guy came up to me during a basketball game and said, 'Earle, would you like to go to college?'

'Sure,' I said, 'I'm planning on it.'

He gave me a card and I put it in my pocket without even glancing at it. When I pulled it out later, I was stunned to see it was from Ohio State. Imagine, Ohio State—interested in me! I filled out the card and called the name on it, Mr. Jammer.

He was one of Ohio State's 'committeemen.' I never knew his first name and had never seen him before that night. He was responsible for a certain territory of the country and finding the top talent for football. He arranged to take me and my teammate, Jim Ruehl, on an 'official' visit to Ohio State. Waiting for that visit was worse than any kid's anticipation for Christmas.

**I'LL ALWAYS REMEMBER MY VISIT.** We arrived at night and I pulled up to that stadium—THE Stadium—the biggest stadium I'd ever seen. It was like pulling up to one of the ancient wonders of the world. There were the great pyramids, the Hanging Gardens of Babylon—and Ohio Stadium. There were lots of office lights on, people moving about, but not a lot of noise. There was almost a hush surrounding the place. It was like a sleeping giant that you shouldn't disturb.

I was young, and I couldn't quite figure out what this weird aura was. I walked around it, trying to take it all in without looking like a total fool country kid. I stretched my neck trying to get a full view. I could have been in the middle of New York City, gazing at skyscrapers. I had never seen a building like this. Although I didn't know it at the time, the stadium had sucked me in. One way or the other, I was going to be part of this place.

Two things impressed me: One was that Wes Fesler, the head coach, walked in and called me 'Lefty,' which was my nickname from high school. I was called 'Lefty' after an outstanding pitcher at our school called 'Lefty' Lee. I'm not left-handed and never have been, but nicknames have rules of their own, and so I was dubbed 'Lefty.' And the head coach of Ohio State knows this. Coach Fesler picked up on that right away.

The second thing was that on my birthday I got a telegram saying 'Happy birthday.'

I immediately wanted to come to Ohio State. At Ohio State, no one called us into a hotel room to size us up. Everyone knew our names. The coaches never talked about my size, instead they talked about my speed. They said I could probably play wingback, because they used a single wing.

**I LOVED OHIO STATE** from the first minute I saw it. There was an aura over the entire place. Maybe it was the stadium. It was like a coliseum. I thought it would be like playing at the top of the world. It was all I wanted to do.

At practice, *jeez*, the freshman team was five deep. Vic Janowicz was the sophomore tailback, and a year away from becoming the first junior to win the Heisman. I wasn't worried about him, because at any moment I might have four good tailbacks ahead of me, and they were all *freshmen*.

I was more intimidated by the single-wing, though, mostly because I didn't know anything about it. After a week or two, I began to learn it, and then I really liked it because it gave me the ball. I was still fast. I was one of the two fastest guys on the team. Walt Klevay was the other.

The freshmen weren't eligible then, and all we did was provide cannon fodder for the varsity. Every day. Sometimes, they'd throw you onto the defensive team. Other days, I'd be on the scout team, running the opponent's plays against the varsity defense. That was when the stadium could have been a coliseum, and I might have been an early Christian, standing in front of the varsity lions.

O my God, you think, maybe I'll never play. You think about transferring. Almost everybody thinks about this at first. The turf is always greener on some other school's pasture. But I still felt like I could play. I was still fast. There was only one other player as fast as me—Walt Klevay—and we were step-for-step. I thought I might be headed for a flanker, or a wide-out position.

Then, in August of 1951—Woody's first year—we were running sweeps, and as I cut, I slipped on the grass and twisted my knee. The trainers thought I pulled a muscle, but instead it was a cartilage. My career was over. The meniscus was torn away from the bone. Now, the knee probably could have been saved, but back then, it was a career-ending event.

**I HAD THOUGHT OF NOTHING BUT PLAYING,** and now everything was over. I didn't know what to do. I don't imagine I was thinking much at all. I wasn't thinking much about an education. I had gone there to play *football*. That is how a young man thinks sometimes, in the moment. Tomorrow is an eternity off.

Giving up the game I loved and the OSU program—it was just too much. I packed up to move back to Cumberland. But when Woody heard of my plans, he sent an assistant coach, Harry Strobel, out to get me. I had left for home already. When I got home, my mother said Coach Strobel had called and said Coach Hayes expected me to come back and finish my education and—help coach the team.

In those days, once you were hurt, you were done. You had to forfeit your aid. So I asked my mom if she was sure she got the message correct. She assured me she had, so I came back to Columbus and the coaches said, 'A deal's a deal.' As long as I did what I was supposed to do, they said, I could keep my work study.

No one did that in those days. You were injured, that was it. But Woody did it routinely. No one else did. Think of it! Someone calls and brings you back from the dead. It was as if I had been resurrected.

I worked with the team as kind of a graduate assistant, without the formal title. I still wasn't sure about coaching as a career. I was considering law school and the FBI. Meanwhile, the FBI changed their requirements, mandating more of an accounting background. That shift in FBI criteria helped convince me the best route for me might be coaching.

I transferred out of the Arts College into Health and Physical Education after spring quarter of my freshman year in 1950. Staying in school at Ohio State and helping coach was a great opportunity. Coaching wasn't like work. Woody's staff made it look like fun. Their influence, coupled with the great high school coaches I had, became the deciding force in choosing to coach. I wanted to be like them.

**I HAD VERY LITTLE RESPONSIBILITY** as a student assistant. I helped out on the field when I could and tried to give some of the younger players some tips and pointers based on my experience. But I think Woody viewed my work as a way to say, 'You're earning your scholarship.' I wasn't really a part of the coaching staff and I definitely wasn't a part of the team, so I tried to stay out of the way on game days, standing with the freshmen and watching the games.

Although I didn't play football at Ohio State, coaching the sport found its way into my blood. Shortly before graduation, I began searching for a high school coaching job. I landed my first interview in Marion, Ohio. On the day of the interview, Woody told me to take his car.

I said, 'Coach, I can't drive your car.'

He asked me how I was planning on getting there and I said I wasn't sure. I planned to ask a fraternity brother or a friend to drive me because I didn't have a car.

Then he *told* me to take his car and get up there to be interviewed. So, there I was, driving to Marion in Coach Hayes' private car. I wasn't a player. I was absolutely nothing in the whole scheme of things, but he took care of me. Although I didn't know it then, Woody would be a factor in every job I would ever hold.

I didn't get the job in Marion. They wanted someone with a little more coaching experience. They didn't want to take a chance on me.

My OSU physical education advisor, Chalmers Hixon, told me about a job in Mansfield, Ohio. He sent me to see an old friend of his, who was the athletic director at Mansfield Senior High School, and he hired me as the offensive and defensive backfield coach. I started work August 20, 1953, while I was finishing a summer school course at OSU, including Woody's course on football. I graduated from Ohio State on August 30, 1953. I was on my own for the first time.

I was a single guy with no ties and Coach Bill 'Pete' Peterson made the most of my lonely status by working my butt off. Every night he called me in to look at film. I then spliced the film to make the highlights film, and I made the team notebook. Pete taught me one thing—hard work. Oh Jesus, college never taught me what ten and twelve hour days were. Now I had a taste of the real thing.

**AFTER THE HIGH SCHOOL DAY ENDED**, Pete gave me every coaching duty possible. I was the junior varsity coach and I'd be with them on Saturday. I'd take the varsity team to the movies on Thursday night to allow the married coaches time with their families. Because I was single, I was nominated to do just about anything. And, I got to coach the best football player to ever come out of Mansfield, Willie Mack. He was all-everything. There wasn't anything Willie Mack couldn't do. He played halfback and defensive safety. He was a kid you had to play games with. When we had a passing scrimmage, I'd tell him I'd give him a break after he made five interceptions. If he was in the right mood—*BOOM!*— he'd start picking them off right and left. A gifted basketball player as well, he was 5' 10" and could jump over the rim and stuff the basketball. He was as good as he wanted to be, and he was probably my greatest high school player.

Coach Peterson was with the program for two years and we were 7-2-1 and 9-1. Our only loss that second year was to Massillon, 18-0, and we should *never* have lost to Massillon. We were a better football team, but they beat us. It was a torrential downpour and Massillon wore special all-weather pants that were rubberized to keep the players dry. Can you imagine that? Once the mud would get on those pants, it just slid right off. It was like our kids were trying to tackle an ice cube.

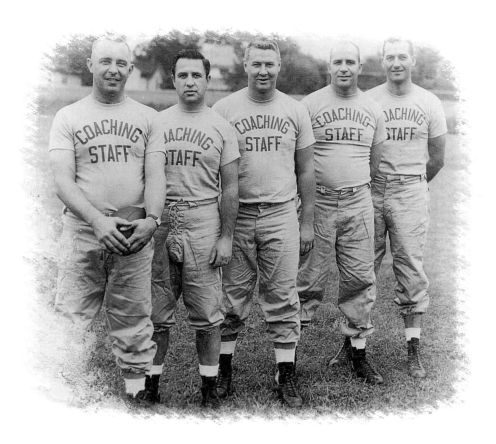

↪*Prep brain trust: Earle (at left) as Salem head coach, where he was 28-9*

The next year, Bob McNea came in to succeed Coach Peterson and we were 8-1-1 and Massillon tied us 12-12. We really outplayed them in their own stadium. Willie Mack ran for over l55 yards. It was his final year and he went to Bowling Green but didn't make the grade academically. Years later, I recruited and coached Willie Mack's son at Iowa State.

My very first coaching job was a great training ground. I don't think Mansfield has ever enjoyed a more successful three years than the Peterson-McNea era. It was a privilege to be an assistant coach for those guys. It was also where I met Jean French. She was a senior, I was a first-year teacher, and she brought me the attendance sheets. When she graduated we began to date, and we were married the next August.

After my third year at Mansfield, I heard about a head football coaching vacancy at Salem High, in northeast Ohio. Again, Woody Hayes was a major factor in my career. Woody's dad was a good friend of the superintendent in Salem, and once Woody put in a good word for me, I was in.

The night before the interview, I had the worst headache in the world. It was a combination of stress, pressure, and worry. But in spite of my pounding head, I did a pretty good job with the school board, and I was hired. They hadn't had a winning record in football at Salem for several years, and they wanted someone to come in and turn the program around. I was their guy.

**OUR FIRST YEAR WAS PRETTY TOUGH.** We went 4-5 in 1956, but we had some good players advancing through the program. Two players moved in because they wanted to play at Salem. We were having some success and becoming a school that was good at athletics. One moved in from Columbiana and the other from Green and it was pretty obvious their talent was a notch above the other kids.

Those two move-ins, Ron Janovic and Don Davidson, were absolutely tremendous football players and 1957 through 1959, we went 9-1, 7-2, and 8-1. We also had Henry Maxim, a super high school fullback/ linebacker, who made interceptions and other plays that were unheard of in high school football. He was Mr. Salem football.

We were playing Brookfield High School, and he raced down the field on the opening kickoff and tackled the kick returner—hard. Then he came to the bench and grabbed some tape.

'What are you doing?' I asked him.

'I think I broke my thumb,' he said.

I advised him to see the doctor.

'If I go talk to him,' Henry said, 'he'll tell me I can't play anymore. No one is going to tell me I'm not going to play anymore!'

Then he simply rolled the tape around his thumb and played the rest of the game.

One of the games I remember was a game when we trailed

Youngstown East 18-0 at halftime and came back in the second half to win 19-18. Do you know what that does for you and your team to win in a comeback situation?

Woody had a tough time coming from behind because he'd normally blow a fuse. His way of winning was to get a 14-0 lead and sit on it. It was always tough for him to put it together if the team fell behind. Even as a young coach I was developing my own instincts of how to stage a comeback. After winning that game 19-18, we had life. And, we had confidence.

The team was earning increased recognition around the state. We were ranked in the top 20 in Ohio my last two seasons and we were able to scrimmage some of the larger schools like Warren. We did pretty well, too, shutting down one of their star players, the great Paul Warfield.

No Ohio team defeated us during my last year at Salem. We had six or eight shutouts. The only team to beat us was from Ambridge, Pennsylvania. The 1959 team still holds the winningest record in Salem football history. To this day, I'm still close with those Salem players.

**IN 1960, I WENT TO SANDUSKY.** During my four seasons at Sandusky, I compiled a record of 33-3-3. The most vivid memory about the kids at Sandusky is speed. Speed kills, and boy, did we have kids who could fly. When our kids ran outside and turned the corner, all they could see was the scoreboard.

We had a fullback by the name of Stewart 'Bug' Williams. He played three years as a fullback and linebacker. He was big and strong at 6' 3" and 235 pounds. When we ran the the 100-yard dash at Buckeye Conference track meets, he was the third guy to finish, even with his 235-pound frame. We had a great championship game against Lorain Admiral King. It was pouring rain and Stewart Williams scored all the points—five touchdowns and five extra points. Defensively, we played an over-shifted defense to keep Stewart on Lorain Admiral King's top running back.

The kids told me that on the first play, Stewart hit their running back, laid on top of him, and said, 'You don't run tonight.'

He repeated it a little louder for some extra emphasis. 'YOU DON'T RUN TONIGHT.'

And the kid didn't.

Eventually, he played at Bowling Green State University and was drafted by the Green Bay Packers. Another kid, Ben Espy, who would go on to star at Ohio State and rise to prominence in Ohio politics, played right halfback.

My favorite story about Ben Espy, involved his release from the hospital after he had been dehydrated from the flu. He left the hospital on Thursday before a huge Friday game with Findlay. He was to accompany the team to the game even though he wasn't going to play. He was just going to suit up.

With the score tied in the fourth quarter, I put him in the game straight off the bench, and he ran for two touchdowns the first two times he touched the ball—45 and 55 yards. Benny Espy had played only two years of football. The year before that, he was in the band.

**WHILE COACHING AT SANDUSKY**, we were always ranked in Ohio's top 10. I was fortunate to have been picked Ohio High School Coach of the Year in 1960. We were number one in the state in 1960. We lost the final game to Marion, costing us the state championship. But our overall record of 33-3-3 still felt great. I know a lot of high school coaches who would take that record and run.

In early 1964, I got a call from the Massillon school superintendent asking if I would be interested in discussing the head football coaching job at Massillon. I really wasn't interested because things were on a roll in Sandusky. But I drove to Elyria and met with the Superintendent privately. I thought I was going to be offered the job and I told him I wasn't really interested.

Shortly after I returned to Sandusky, my phone rang, and it was Woody. Carl 'Ducky' Schroeder, the legendary Massillon assistant, had called Woody and told him to call me.

'You can't turn that Massillon job down!' Woody said.

'Woody,' I said, 'I'm going to have the greatest team that Sandusky's ever had. We've got great football up here. Massillon couldn't beat us! We scrimmaged 'em and knocked their jocks off.'

'Earle,' Woody said, 'you'd better look at that job a little harder. You can't go wrong. You're going to be the athletic director and it's all there right in front of you.'

As always, Woody made me think. I decided that maybe I should arrange a more thorough interview. To this day, the interview I had at Massillon was the most in-depth interview I ever had. They asked me to bring a highlight film of my team to illustrate the kind of offense and defense I was running. They also wanted to see my notebook, and to explain it and my system. The interviewers wanted you to talk about football. Not just the technical side of the game, they wanted to measure your passion for the sport.

ABOUT A DOZEN PEOPLE were present in the board of education meeting room. School board members were all there, along with members of the boosters club and the community. The experience really impressed me. The prospect of changing jobs was a dilemma. Sandusky had a great program and a great school. Massillon had a great program, but the school was in a state of disrepair. Yet Massillon conducted the best interview process and the best recruiting process I had ever seen.

On April 1, 1964, after much thought, I left my history class at Sandusky High School and decided to go to Massillon. One thing surprised me. When I told the people at Sandusky I was leaving for Massillon, no one fought to keep me. Even with a 33-3-3 record, the administration maintained if they gave me any incentive to stay, they'd have to do likewise for this teacher and that teacher. They weren't willing to set that precedent. So, their decision told me, maybe I had made a good decision.

They said in Massillon that if you lost, the hometown would stone the team bus. They said the first game you lose, they dump a truckload of garbage on your lawn. Some coaches told me that. I don't know if they were perpetuating a myth, or what. I didn't intend to find out whether it was mythology or not. I worked hard to keep the garbage off my lawn.

And Massillon really lived up to its reputation of being the cream of the high school football crop. I was not only the head football coach, but athletic director, and in charge of physical education in both junior and senior high. I also ran all the intramural programs. I had an assistant, facility manager Roger Price, to take care of all the overflow.

I wore a lot of titles, and took home a $11,000 salary and a brand new car every year. I taught a history class and had regular lunch duty. All my other time was needed to concentrate on football. Principal I. W. Snyder tried to force another study hall on me once, but it wasn't in my contract.

As a football coach, the perks available for your team were only limited by your imagination. Roger would sit down with me and say, 'Hey, would you like some special uniforms for this game?' Or, 'How about a free dinner for the kids that come to weight training ninety per cent or 100 per cent of the time?'

'We can do that?' I asked him.

'Oh, yes,' he said, 'we can do just about anything you'd like.'


**I CHOSE TO STAY ON THE CONSERVATIVE SIDE.** But there was no limit to incentives if it helped the kids and contributed to the success of the program. We hired two guys to help run the conditioning program at the stadium during the summer, and paid 'em good money. As long as we could justify that it would help us win, we never had any problem getting it done. You don't get that kind of cooperation everywhere.

In 1964, the first thing that knocked me out about Massillon football was the level of intensity from the kids. In most schools I coached, you had six guys on the defensive team really going after it and hitting. At Massillon, all eleven came all at once on every play and hit your ass and knocked you flat. And they played from the opening gun until the end of the game. They never gave up.

The first game of the year we played Cleveland East. It was a close game, and I kept thinking how short my career at Massillon would be. The scoreboard said 0-0 with less than two minutes in the game. Somehow we won, 16-0. Cleveland East's fullback, Jim Pledger, was running crazy against us. Fortunately for us, their halfback fumbled on the nine-yard line. That mistake allowed us to force the ball in on fourth and 2 to score and get ahead 8-0. They got the ball back, threw a pass, we intercepted it, returned it for a touchdown, and the story had a 16-0 ending.

*Catching up: Rick Paige with winning touchdown pass, snapping 48-game streak by Niles*

The next night, I scouted our upcoming opponent, Niles McKinley. They won 49-0 over Cleveland East Tech. East Tech had punched those Niles kids after every play and finally, Niles had enough. They exploded and beat the devil out of Tech. I couldn't believe it. I thought, boy, do we have our hands full against Niles.

We played the following week in Akron's Rubber Bowl before a sellout crowd of more than 30,000 in a cool drizzle. Even ol' Ducky Schroeder's wife, Gert, thought we would lose that game. She wasn't quite sure exactly what kind of coach I was just yet.

I always said that was the night I became a Tiger. Boy, did our kids play defense. Our quarterback, Dave Sheggog, also played cornerback and he made tackles right and left. One of our guys, receiver Rick Paige, was in jail until right before the game. He was released in time to play the game and scored the winning touchdown. I drew up the game-winning touchdown to Rick Paige on the sideline. He'd caught the out cut about five times during the game, and I asked him if he could run the same route, just turn up the field this time.

I drew it on the sideline with some of the boosters in the stands watching me draw the play. Normally we only ran plays we'd practiced numerous times, but Rick had been in jail instead of practice. I told him he'd be wide open and would walk right into the end zone.

Rick told me he could run the route and he did—the pass was right there—and he walked in for the winning score, 14-8.

IN SEVEN OF THE TEN GAMES we played that year we were either tied or behind in the fourth quarter but managed to win 'em all. That's how hard the kids of Massillon played football. After beating Niles we were ranked number one in the state.

At the Tuesday night practice, I told 'em, 'This is the seventh week in a row we're ranked number one. Who would have thought that we'd be in this position ten weeks ago?'

'WE ALL DID, WE ALL DID,' they shouted and cheered.

I thought to myself, Holy shit, go on in boys, you don't need any more of a pep talk from me. *I* was the guy who had to find out how to deal with being number one. *They* expected it!

These remarkable kids came at every opponent as a team and proved their character in the season-ending game against arch-rival Canton McKinley. The team was down 14-0 in the fourth quarter and scored 20 straight points to win. Sheggog scored almost all 20 points by himself, running the option, even returning a punt down to the three-yard line.

I told him to watch out for a crazy bounce by the ball. *Leave it alone!* I said. He jumped up and caught it with one huge hand and sprinted off to put us in position to win the game. The only disappointing part of the year was our final ranking of number two in the nation, behind Coral Gables, Florida. There was no way that school would have beaten our kids.

**VOLUMES HAVE BEEN WRITTEN** about sports tradition in college, but I don't think there is more tradition anywhere—on any level—than in Massillon. The great booster clubs—the Sideliners, Reese's Raiders, Quarterback Club, Massillon Boosters Club, there were always 700 to 800 people in the school auditorium to talk football with the coach every week. And, that kind of support went on all year. I had experienced a great booster club in Salem and Sandusky as well, but nothing compared to the community involvement in Massillon.

I loved to sit down with the boosters club members and listen to their tales about hiding guys in the scoreboard in Canton and staying overnight to watch McKinley's practices. One example of the zealousness of the Tiger Town boosters involved a game played in Altoona, Pennsylvania.

About 3,000 fans traveled to the game by train. Before the game, assistant coach Ducky Schroeder said, 'Hey, Coach, the boosters club has been in our locker room, planning a little surprise to get the kids fired up. They planted a microphone. If you just play along, everything will be great.'

The unveiling of the stunt began during pregame warm-ups as assistant coach John Behling and our trainer came running out onto the field, yelling to me, 'They wired our dressing room. They WIRED our dressing room. There's a microphone. We saw it.'

I said, 'Don't touch it, just leave it there. I'll take care of it when I come in and don't tell anyone.'

So we're in the locker room preparing to take the field and I'm giving them the pre-game speech when I turned around, spotted the microphone hanging down from the ceiling, and exploded, 'Oh my God, they've wired our dressing room.'

With that, I pulled the microphone and the cord out from the ceiling. The players didn't seem too upset about it. Ironically, my cousin started the frenzy for real after hearing my announcement, by running out the door and up into the stands telling all the Massillon fans that our dressing room was bugged.

He's running up and down the aisles in the stands yelling, 'They wired the dressing room! They wired the dressing room! Can you imagine those sonofabitches wired the dressing room!'

Boy, was he worked up. Now, most everyone in the stands knows the inside story on the 'wired' dressing room. Our equipment manager saw a couple of Altoona guys standing between the dressing rooms and yelled, 'You sonofabitches wired our dressing room!'

The Altoona people became pretty indignant and we go out and win the game 12-0. I was told after the game the 'wiring' incident really helped motivate our team. As we entered the locker room after the game, those same three Altoona guys our manager had confronted before the game introduced themselves to Ducky. One was the principal, one the superintendent, and one was the athletic director.

'We understand you had a problem before the game and we want to find out what happened because we will not tolerate that from our coach,' they said. 'Was there a microphone in your locker room?'

Ducky had the microphone in his pocket and said, 'Oh, no…no, that, that…don't worry about that…that's nothing.'

They were ready to fire their coach, Earl Strom. He was a real stand up guy, and we had to do a lot of backpedaling to try and save his job. Ducky came over to me and asked what to do.

'Get rid of the microphone,' I said.

**OUR BOOSTERS CLUB** used to drop pamphlets about the other team where our kids could find them. They'd also put club members up in the trees around our practice field with binoculars to give the impression the opponent was spying and gathering information on the Tigers. Think about that. These are *adults* doing this stuff.

We did have a real 'spy' once from Mansfield. The 'Reese's Raiders' booster group used to provide security during practice and patrol the football field. One day, a Mansfield spy was discovered and our boosters chased the guy all the way to the city limits.

I did my part by calling Mansfield's head football coach and said, 'Hey, we just put your guy in jail. The police over here are very cooperative when someone tries to spy on our practices. Hear me. He's in JAIL.'

Can you imagine what happened for the next hour before that guy made it back to Mansfield? It would have been great fun to watch them stew and wait to see if we were bluffing.

I was so proud to drive that white station wagon with orange and black trim that said, 'Massillon Tigers.' The 'Obie' mascot was on the side, and the words 'Massillon, Ohio—City of Champions' on the back.

Once I drove to Lake Wales, Florida, to see a coaching buddy of mine. His school administrator was so impressed with the visibility a car like that provided that my buddy wound up getting a car from his school, too.

ONCE, I WAS DRIVING HOME through Valdosta, Georgia, and two guys begin chasing me up the street yelling, 'We're the Massillon of the south, we're the Massillon of the south!'

I stopped the car and they came over to me and said, 'We ARE the Massillon of the south,' and I said, 'What do you mean?'

'Well,' they said, 'we've got the reputation down here. We've got the program. We're known all over Georgia.'

I'll never forget those two guys so anxious to compare Valdosta, Georgia, with our program in Massillon. I would have loved to have scheduled their team against ours, but at that time we weren't allowed to schedule teams from all over the country. We could schedule in Pennsylvania, Kentucky, or Indiana because they were adjacent states. Actually we didn't need the exposure—Massillon on its own was larger than life.

Our off season was sprinkled with constant workouts and a lot of hard work by our junior high players in the spring. We had a kid at

Jones Jr. High school named Jim Smith. He would later go on and score a lot of touchdowns for the Tigers, but coaches found him a little tough to handle. I loved kids like Jim Smith. I could relate to them. I always put in extra effort at working with them, and it was always important to me that those kids saw something positive in what they did. They weren't math geniuses and they were brought up a little differently, but I enjoyed the challenge of finding what made them tick.

We had another great prospect coming up, a fullback named Will Foster. God, he was really good. He played linebacker and ran right halfback. He was big as a horse and when he hit you as a linebacker, you knew you were hit. We had a great halfback from the famous James family in Massillon, Tommy James.

OUR TALENT WAS STACKING UP and the future looked good. We had some close ball games that second year at Massillon. We won at Steubenville in a close ball game, 18-14. The game was especially memorable that year because some of their kids urinated on our cheerleaders. From the *stands*.

That fired up all of Massillon. We won a close ball game at home against Warren with a fumble recovery on what should have been their game-winning drive. We came from behind again 14-0 against Canton McKinley at McKinley.

I told Ducky Schroeder at halftime, 'Hey, Ducky, you can't come from behind two years in a row against Canton McKinley. No one does that. We're gonna get our butts beat.'

'Don't you give up!' he said.

'I'm not giving up,' I said. 'But being realistic, it's 14-0 and they're playing well. We're not playing very well, Ducky.'

We come out of the locker room at Fawcett Stadium in Canton and there outside our door, going the length of the field, were two rows of the entire student body, welcoming the team back onto the field. They weren't supposed to be out there, but no one could stop them. We ran through them and you could feel the energy take over your body.

I thought, 'If they haven't given up, what the hell am *I* doing giving up?'

So we got together before the second half and became a different team. Tommy James intercepted a pass and ran it back into McKinley territory to get us started, and we won the game 18-14 when Will Foster ran nearly twenty yards on what we called the 17, a power off tackle.

Foster made the game-winning touchdown by picking up a key first down on a hook pass from Dave Sheggog. From my line of vision, I didn't think he ran the route correctly, and I was yelling and screaming because I thought we were short on yardage.

We did what was necessary to win that season. Back then, that All-American football conference was tough. Alliance, Canton McKinley, Warren, Niles, Steubenville, all were programs to be wary of. It was a good league, with a lot of emotion and physical play each week. But no one had more support and tradition than Massillon.

I never lost a game at Massillon—twenty wins. There was another coach who had an unbeaten season, but he had five tie games. So I say I was their only undefeated, untied coach.

**THE LESSONS I LEARNED IN MASSILLON** have stayed with me all my life. It is one of the purest football environments I'm aware of. Young coaches know that if you want a career in high school coaching, don't go to Massillon. Massillon has always been viewed as a stepping stone to college football. The boosters don't want you to stay. They love it when former coaches excel from Massillon roots. The community likes to brag about all their coaches who joined college programs—Chuck Mather, Leo Strang, Jim Tressel, Tom Harp.

If you are too successful in Massillon it will be time to move on. Success was part of the trouble with Coach Mike Currence at Massillon back in the '80s. Once he got a little too close to Paul Brown's record, he was gone. At Massillon, you can't buck tradition.

# The master

Coaching high school fo o t b a l l taught me real things about the game. I'd mastered the essentials of blocking and tackling and had begun to appreciate the importance of teaching and discipline, performance, hard work, and loyalty. Looking back now, I realize I was still a naïve kid.

➲ *The Man: A characteristic pose along the sidelines for a quarter of a century*

My real coaching education had yet to begin.

In May of 1964 ,Ohio State assistant coach Lou

McCullough told me of an opening on Woody's staff.

Max Urich, the defensive secondary coach, was

having some problems with Woody and decided

to move on. Now, I knew *everyone* had problems

with Woody so I wasn't deterred at all from being

interested in the position.

———

Woody was looking for a new defensive backs coach and I was being considered, along with Canton McKinley head coach, Don Nehlen. Although Don was a strong candidate, he had one big problem. He wanted Sundays off to attend church. Woody wouldn't even consider such an idea. It wasn't that Woody wasn't religious. Woody wanted everyone to *work* religiously. Woody simply believed we all had too much to do to be able to afford a day off—ever. We never even knew if we'd have Christmas Day off.

Lou McCullough alerted me that I was still in the running, but it was all up to Woody. The coach and I had kept in contact over the years, so he knew where to find me. I was asked to come to Columbus for an interview on a Sunday. Woody didn't normally ask you in unless he was going to hire you. Here I was for the first time talking formally with

Woody in his office—as a coach, not as a player. This was a little different. I was afraid he'd think I didn't know very much about coaching. I wanted him to view me as up and coming, knowledgeable about the game, not his former player or a young kid who was still wet behind the ears. I really wanted the job, but I didn't feel like I'd get it.

We had lunch at his favorite place, the old Jai Lai on Olentangy River Road. We talked about the position, but he never tried to sell me on the job. Instead, he spent most of lunch pointing out some less desirable aspects. He described the recruiting headaches, the long hours, how tough he was to work for. He never mentioned any holidays off or vacation time. He gave all the minuses in great detail.

Before his plate was totally clean, he offered me the job. I knew immediately I was going to accept. I was jumping into the big time for the whopping salary of $11,000 a year. I knew it would be either the biggest thrill of my life or the greatest mistake.

It was also my first job on the defensive side of the ball. Woody told me that if something opened up on offense, I could move to that side of the ball. I had stayed current on the latest defensive secondary schemes by being at Massillon. As a matter of fact, Massillon was ahead of Ohio State in defensive pass coverage strategies.

Ohio State was playing three deep cold-zone defense and not doing anything. At Massillon, we were rolling and playing man and mixing up our coverages. We used the stuff we learned in clinics and copied the plays the pros were showing, and it was a part of our system.

IT WAS DIFFICULT TO LEAVE MASSILLON. I did find comfort through a conversation with assistant football coach Ducky Schroeder. 'You can't leave here for some place like Miami of Ohio as an assistant coach,' he said. 'You'd have to go there as a head coach. But going to Ohio State as an assistant coach, that's okay.'

His take on the move meant a lot to me. I left, knowing the people of Massillon would understand. I finished high school coaching with a record of 82-12-3. But it was still tough to leave a place the caliber of Massillon where you were top dog and head off to a new position where you'd be living at the bottom of the barrel.

I took a pay cut to work for Woody. At first he said, 'I can't afford you.' My negotiating didn't go well from that point on. My job was worth $13,000, the same salary I'd been receiving in Massillon. After I accepted the job at $11,000 he said, 'I'll try to get you $11,500.'

I left everything, paid my own moving expenses, and came to Columbus for $11,000. I ripped open my first paycheck to see if he got me the $11,500. It was for $11,000. He could have gotten me $11,500 just by snapping his fingers. But Woody didn't care a bit about money. I couldn't believe I'd been offered $11,000 as an assistant to Bo Schembechler at Miami of Ohio. I had turned that offer down the previous month and here I was with the same money at Ohio State. I was taking a pay cut to leave high school and coach college ball.

Woody's frugal style taught me a valuable lesson. When I became a head coach I would ask an assistant his salary requirements. If he said $32,000, I'd tell him he had his $32,000. Then when he received his first paycheck, he'd see a little extra. Maybe I had bumped his salary just a little— say to $34,000.

Almost every guy came in and said, 'Thanks, coach.' That way, the assistant started out knowing he was someone special. He got a bonus before he even started. He goes home and tells his wife about it. They both feel good about the job. I knew this little trick helped everyone stay happy from day one.

**BUT THAT WASN'T WOODY'S PHILOSOPHY.** He wanted you to struggle a little bit. He used to tell us, 'A pat on the back weakens you, a kick in the ass toughens you up.' And he sure gave you a lot more kicks in the ass than he did pats on the back.

I lived payday to payday and I survived because I loved what I was doing. During my years with Woody, I worked with the defensive secondary and the offensive line, which are the two most important assistant positions in football. You don't dare give up big plays in the defensive backfield and the offensive line better move 'em off the ball or you don't win the game.

In that first year as a defensive secondary coach, I really had to double my efforts because spring ball was already over. I was hired the second week of May and reported for work on July 1. I spent a lot of time looking at film and getting organized.

What a staff we had. Bill Mallory was the defensive line coach, Lou McCullough was defensive coordinator and linebacker coach, and Esco Sarkkinen was the defensive ends coach. On offense, Harry Strobel was guards and centers coach, Hugh Hindman was tackles and tight ends, Rudy Hubbard was backfield coach, Larry Catuzzi was the quarterbacks coach and, of course, Woody was the offensive coordinator. Bo Rein worked as a non-paid assistant with the wide receivers.

OH, WHAT AN EXPERIENCE. We'd meet every morning at 8 a.m. and get organized for the day. Then we'd break into offense and defense. Woody stayed mostly with the offense, so I hardly saw him. Defensive coaches never really knew Coach Hayes the way offensive coaches knew him. Our hours started at 8 a.m. and ended at 10 or 11 at night.

We worked out of St. John Arena before Woody moved the football staff to the North Facility along Olentangy River Road. Once we moved into the North Facility, Woody became a hermit. He never went back to main campus or to St. John Arena where the other athletic coaches and administrators were. He stayed to himself. He'd dismiss us everyday at 11 or 12, then take a little cat-nap while we got the playbook and schedule made and prepared for practice.

I always said if I became a head coach, I'd turn it into an 8 to 5 job. Then when I did, I discovered it *wasn't* an 8 to 5 job. You come in at 7:30 or 8 a.m., meet and prepare for practice, practice, de-brief from practice, then go to the training table. We always ate with the players at training table. As head coach I ate with our players every night except Thursday night. It was my one night to go home and eat with my family.

As Woody's assistant, you went back to the office after training table

⊃*Bo and Earle: A little sideline exchange before the day's business begins*

and did more work. Preparation was the key to a successful football season. If you've got your practice plan set for Monday, Tuesday, and Wednesday, that's called 'organization.' When teams are always adding and subtracting and changing things, it's a signal the team is in trouble. It's not unusual to put in a play here and there, but you can't keep changing your offense in big ways. If you're doing that, you're losing.

Woody always said he wasn't as smart as the next guy, but he'd sure out work whoever *was* smartest. He lived by that creed. We spent a lot more time than other teams on planning and preparation, and I'm not sure it was all necessary. We spent a huge amount of time planning contingencies. Instead of sitting around for hours at a time and debating plays, which we did, we could have been more resolute.

As defensive coaches, our number one task was to look at the opponent and see how to stop him. If we decided to add anything to the play book, it was added early in the week to allow plenty of time to practice it. Normally, we'd add anything new on Monday and practice it Monday and Tuesday. If the new stuff didn't work out, those plays would be gone by Wednesday.

We were always looking for that special edge, and sometimes we'd find it and sometimes we didn't. We'd waste a lot of time looking for that mysterious 'edge' before we settled down to the week's game plan. Our cardinal rule was, if you could execute it in practice, then you could execute it in the game. If you couldn't execute it in practice, you probably weren't going to execute it in the game.

**ON DEFENSE, IF YOU KEEP YOUR KIDS** in good football position so they make plays and run to the ball, then you'll be okay. There were certain other cardinal rules we had to follow under Woody. You never, EVER, put the fullback into the 'boundary.'

In the late '50s and early '60s, the fullback played both ways. He usually fit the perfect profile for a defensive back or 'rover back,' as we came to call the position. Later of course, we recruited players specifically for the 'rover back' position. Under Woody's law, you always had to keep him on the wide side of the field to defend against the breakaway run, the sweep to the open side of the field. That came from his military strategy of keeping the right flank strong.

If the rover back was out of position and the opponent threw deep (heaven forbid a touchdown), that defensive secondary coach might as well pack his bags. He'd be gone. Our strategy was to give up the short pass, but always guard against the 'home run.'

I remember being on the sideline one time when we were playing Wisconsin. They were using a flood pattern and we were playing a 3-and-3 on the defensive end, and they came at us with a slot back and we were out of position. Our rover back wasn't fast enough to get back into the hook area to cover the slot back's curl. They completed it five times and Woody said to me, 'When are you going to stop that play?'

I said, 'I'm going to stop it when I can move my fullback to where he has to be. The kid can't be where you want him to be and cover that curl route. If you want to move him over to the slot back, fine, and then I can drop a back. But if you want to stop the run and play 3-and-3 on an uncovered end, then I got a problem and they'll throw that curl all day long. You've got an impossible situation and the poor kid can't function.' I knew I was pushing my luck with Coach.

I brought my coaching ideas to Woody before I knew any better. I tried to make a point with him one day about 'dropping the end.' I wanted to drop the defensive end into a spot as outside linebacker.

'Drop the end—you're gone!' Woody said. We did it his way, of course.

**'YOU'RE EITHER FISH OR A FOWL,'** Woody would say, meaning when you drop the end, you're not a linebacker and you're not a defensive back. He didn't believe in that. There was no arguing—he always won. We were just talking football. But he didn't want to hear that—period.

Now coaches drop the defensive end and the tackle has the contain, but you never did that under Woody. We were always a little limited by what Woody would allow us to do. When we had great athletes to work with, Woody's rigid beliefs were not a problem. But when we *didn't* have the great athlete, or if they weren't in perfect position, we had trouble. The kids couldn't function in some situations because Woody wouldn't give an inch on his philosophies.

Woody's ways were a constant topic during the hours spent in our defensive staff meetings. We dropped a defensive end as an outside linebacker one time in a game and when Sark saw the action he came back and screamed, 'You'll get me fired! You'll get me fired! Don't ever drop that end again!' That's the way it was. That's why Ohio State went to the 4-3 defense.

Woody always held us responsible and I never had a problem with that. But Woody also believed that you could teach every kid to do any task. In reality, you can't ask a kid to do something he's not capable of doing. If they don't have speed, if they can't bend their legs, they can't make the play. Talent cannot be taught and athletes have differing degrees of talent.

That was a little bit of a difference between Woody and me. I'm not criticizing Coach Hayes because I understand his intent, but sometimes I just didn't agree.

**THAT FIRST YEAR WASN'T VERY GOOD.** We were 4 and 5 in 1966. As a defensive assistant, I often thought we had better players at defensive end in Massillon than we had at Ohio State. We had great kids, but we weren't bursting with skilled athletes. We didn't have great running or defensive backs. We had a lot of kids at the defensive back position who were former wide receivers with injuries.

Woody gave us all $300 raises after that season, which I think was the lowest raise ever given to an assistant coach at Ohio State. That was his way of telling us we weren't doing the job. That was not what Ohio State football was about. The message was loud and clear. We had to do better.

Woody didn't do a lot of yelling and screaming about the season. Once he said his piece, he was out the door. He never hammered you about the same thing every day. What he gauged was your reaction as a coach.

Recruiting was as torturous as Woody had promised. We went from football season until May 20, 1967, recruiting all the way. Imagine that—National Signing Day on May 20. You can't imagine how terrible your life could be as an assistant football coach. I was running from Columbus to Pennsylvania to cover my recruiting territory. I only got one recruit, Jan White, the All-American. Thank God I got him. That kid never knew he saved my life.

We started out 1967 by losing three of the first five games. Our record kept sliding right downhill to 2-2 before Homecoming. We knew if we lost one more game, that might be it for all of us. Things were getting ugly. There were the airplane banners saying, 'So long Woody.'

Then he was hung in effigy from the stadium. Coach Hayes pretended not to notice. He never said a word or acknowledged that anything negative was going on. But we all knew the pressure was mounting on him.

As assistants, we circled the wagons and worked that much harder. The first thing we decided is that we had no Supermen on the team. No kid glove treatment would be given to anyone. Everybody would be treated the same. We didn't talk anymore about potential, only performance.

We narrowed our focus to one thing only—get your ass in gear and produce. The adversity, the challenge, and the discipline drew the team together. Players and coaches alike didn't want anyone saying any nasty things about Coach Hayes. *We* might criticize him, but all that stayed within the team.

I NEVER SAW A TEAM like the one in 1967 come back from adversity. We were 2 and 3 and headed to East Lansing. Public opinion predicted we'd lose to Michigan State but our kids rallied to play one helluva football game. We were up 21-0 before Michigan State could score and the way they scored was to push our safety in the back and catch the football—and no one called it.

Michigan State had a helluva football team that year. When we won that game, we knew we could beat anybody. After winning in East Lansing, we came home and beat Wisconsin and Indiana and then we went to Ann Arbor.

The 1967 Michigan game in Ann Arbor, we really splattered 'em, 24-14. It could have been worse, but Woody sat on the score in the fourth quarter. Rudy Hubbard didn't run the ball all year but he had a helluva game against Michigan. He was a wingback and receiver all season and never really got the ball. But for Michigan, he was sensational.

That game brought tears to my eyes. I was happy for the kids and I knew they couldn't fire us after beating Michigan. All the coaches received $900 raises. What a relief. And we knew that for the next three years, we would have quality football players.

# Championship season

We knew we had assembled exceptional talent after recruiting the 1968 team. The group was ineligible as freshmen, but much of the time they outperformed the varsity team in practice. I had recruited Jan White. Lou McCullough had recruited

*↪Woody and Rex Kern: A pair of champions in search of a championship*

Rex Kern. But Larry Catuzzi was the king of recruiting that year. Tatum, Jankowski, Brockington, and Zelina—to name a few—were the results of his hard work. Assistant Coach Harry Strobel retired, paving the way for me to be moved to the offensive line, just as Woody had promised when I was first hired in 1966. Lou Holtz was hired to replace me as coach of the defensive secondary.

———————————

During spring football in early April of 1968, it became evident that Billy Long, who had played quarterback in 1967, was being beaten out by two of our freshmen, Rex Kern and Ron Maciejowski. Bill did a great job for us. He competed as best he could. I'm sure sliding back to the third team was difficult for him. But it was quickly becoming evident our 'Super Sophomores' were simply better than their older teammates. They had speed and agility. They were smart. Their aptitude for the game and the system allowed them to simply take over. We knew the running backs and defensive backs were going to be outstanding. It was just a matter of getting them all funneled into the same system.

Seventeen of the thirty players we recruited that year started for us in September. Once the season started rolling, everything fell in place. We took SMU and Purdue. We beat Illinois and Iowa in crucial road games.

But there were some big potholes in our road as well. We were ahead of Illinois 24-0 at the half and Woody went into an Abraham Lincoln speech that almost killed us.

He said Abe would have been a great offensive tackle or defensive tackle or tight end. He went on and on about Abe but nothing about game strategy. We thought we'd go back out and score 24 more points and it would be 48-0.

Illinois, however, didn't discuss Abe Lincoln in their locker room at halftime. They had made play adjustments. They split out their right tackle and kept the ball by running their fullback to the right side and we never got the ball back. Illinois scored three touchdowns and three two-point conversions, which made it 24-24. We finally passed a long ball down to the four-yard line, scored in the last minute, and won the game. OSU 31, Abraham Lincoln 24.

Then we went out to Iowa in horrible weather and jumped out to a big lead, 26-6 and all of the sudden, *BOOM*. Iowa comes back and closes the gap to within a couple of points. Ed Podolak ran the ball like the devil for Iowa that day, but we held on and won 33-26.

THE HIGHLIGHT FOR ME IN 1968 was the Michigan game. It was 14-14 at one point and we ended up winning 50 to 14. Our mindset was such that nothing was going to stop us. I remember the sun coming out at halftime after we had gone ahead 21-14. I felt it was a lucky omen.

We could see at halftime our defense was really picking it up. We came out at the start of the third quarter and went up 28-14. When we kicked a field goal to make it 31-14, they gave up. What a game we played! As the game wore into the fourth quarter, we started to sense that we were going to the Rose Bowl.

The Rose Bowl! Lou McCullough and I were dancing around up in the press box, yelling that we're going to the Rose Bowl. Some of the assistant coaches who had been with Woody to the Rose Bowl previously warned us that we had no idea what was in store. His coaches always said

Woody was a lot more humble in defeat than he was in victory.

We flew to California as a team on December 20. My family came out on the 23rd. It was my first Christmas away from home. We practiced every day, and we worked on the game plan. We spent a great deal of effort to make sure the players weren't homesick. When OSU was at a bowl game over the Christmas holiday, the athletic department would host a Christmas party for the football program's 'family'—players, coaches and their wives, athletic department administrators. One of the team members played Santa, skits were presented, some of the players played carols on the piano, and we tried to sing.

Woody wasn't around for the party. He spent the time in seclusion, apparently working on the game. We rarely saw him away from the field. But he allowed the players to call home, a huge concession on his part. His preference was to keep all player telephones disconnected.

Although there were first class activities available to our families, the coaches didn't get to attend many. The Bowl appearance was like a normal day at the office for us. I remember going out to that huge Pasadena stadium for the first time. The San Gabriel mountain range in the background made it look like a postcard. I had never seen anything like it before in my life.

**SOME DISTRACTIONS WERE HARD TO IGNORE.** President Nixon came to that Rose Bowl game. Woody visited with him and I remember many spectators were delayed getting to their seats because of all the extra security needed to get the President and his entourage into the game.

As beautiful as it was on the first of January in Southern California, I couldn't think of anything but the football game. I didn't know how good Southern Cal was but I knew how good we were. I thought to myself, how could we lose? We're not gonna lose. We got behind Southern Cal 10-0, we tied it at 10-10, broke it open for a 26-10 lead. Southern Cal scored a late touchdown after a pass interference call, to make it 26-16.

I had never considered the possibility of losing. I couldn't picture a losing scenario in my mind. There is a lot to be said for that whole philosophy of visualization. The 1968 season made me believe that anything could happen.

Woody was pretty good with those kids all year. He recognized they could play football. They took coaching and got better and better. When everything was going well, Woody left you alone to do your job. But he was always involved. We were in one of those rare time warps, high on success with a group of kids who truly loved to play football.

As good as the 1968 national championship team was, I thought the 1969 team was better. I thought our level of play was better. Our scores were better. Our execution had improved. This was one fine-looking team. The 1969 team was *really* good. I never thought we would lose a game. I held onto that thought throughout twenty-four straight wins. Then came Michigan.

**IT WAS COLD AND SNOWY.** I guess my gut feeling for trouble was reinforced when our team came out of the tunnel and began to warm up at the wrong end of the field. The Michigan fans were livid and snowballed us. The fans got to the stadium early—the place was full for the warm-ups —which is always a sign that the fans and the players are ready for you.

They *were* ready. They remembered last season's game when we went for two to drive the score from 48-14 to 50-14. Michigan was humiliated and that got them all stirred up. And they had a new head coach—Bo Schembechler. He was an Ohio native and our former assistant. He'd come straight from the head coach job at Miami of Ohio to take over at Michigan. Bo pulled out all the stops and his kids were well prepared. Saying Bo had them ready was an understatement. Those kids were like machines.

The only game they lost that season was to Missouri. They won all their other games and were gunning for Ohio State. They were just waiting for us. We had our chances during the game, but we didn't take advantage of them. We made costly mistakes, including five interceptions, which helped us beat ourselves. It had to be Rex Kern's worst game ever, but a loss like that couldn't be blamed on just one player. Michigan won 24-12.

That 1969 game with Michigan turned out to be more significant than most people would guess. The defeat itself became secondary. That game marked the 'unofficial official' start of the 'Woody vs. Bo' era. Bo was a graduate assistant when I was a student. He served as Woody's assistant before accepting the Miami of Ohio head coach job. The stories are legendary about Bo and Woody. It was kind of like the father and son who never got along. The son was always wanting it done his way and fighting his dad tooth and nail.

It was volatile relationship. Woody fired him four or five times during the years he was at Ohio State. But when Bo left Ohio State as an assistant, it was Woody who helped him get the job at Miami. They screamed and yelled at each other all the time, but both had a keen respect for the other. Woody always knew Bo was a good football coach. He also knew how much Bo loved the challenge of competing—not only against Ohio State—but against the 'Old Man.'

Woody knew that Bo wanted to beat him worse than anything else. Woody knew that this would become a personal rivalry as much as a college football rivalry. With an Ohio guy at the helm of the Michigan program, the intensity of the rivalry exploded. Competition extended from the field to recruiting. Several of Bo's assistant coaches had Ohio ties, but none of them were quite like Bo. Woody knew that with Bo at Michigan, he would have his hands full.

We weren't ready to go up there and lose in 1969. I know that. But we didn't realize we were in that hot box until we got there. Little did we know that the hot box had turned into an incinerator. If we had known the intensity of the scene we might have done some things differently to make sure our team was as emotionally charged as the Michigan team and its fans.

The atmosphere that day was different from any other time we had brought a team to Michigan Stadium. As I was walking up the steps to the press box before the game, a fan about five rows up, adorned in maize and blue, grabbed me by the front of my scarlet coaches' jacket and shook me.

'You're gonna get yours today, buddy!' he yelled at me.

I wasn't ready for that. I didn't know what was going on. I climbed another ten or fifteen rows and a Michigan fan jumps up and yells at me, 'We're ready today, buddy. We're gonna beat your ass!'

Imagine that! Two fans in the stands, yelling at an opponent's coach. I thought I'd be in a fight on my way to the press box. I thought, 'Christ, they *are* worked up.'

That's not something you can talk about in your team meetings as you prepare for the game beforehand. You can't truly gauge the emotion of your opponent until game day. It's the same way in Columbus.

 At half time we were behind, but we were confident we could come back. It was all business in the locker room. No screaming and yelling, no fists through the blackboard. In the second half, we had the Wolverines on third and four, running the fullback off-tackle, moving the ball normally. We're driving down the field around the Michigan 20 with the chance to take control of the game, and Woody called the fullback-delay pass.

I'll never forget assistant coach Hugh Hindman yelling, 'No, Woody, NO! We wanna run the ball. If we come up with only two yards, we can make two more on fourth down. We don't want to throw the ball, we just want to run it!'

**THE DELAY PASS FELL INCOMPLETE**. Now, it's fourth and four. We chose to run the option to the closed side of the field. The play was predictable as hell, and Bo's defense stuffed it. It stops our drive deep inside Michigan territory. Sometimes games come down to a single decision. In play calling, you're damned if you do and damned if you don't. Second-guessing! Fans are the only group with the right to be second-guessers. Coaches can't do that. The game was over and there were more than enough mistakes to go around that day.

Selecting the right play at the right time was the responsibility of the coaches. Execution was up to the players. The Michigan team reacted well to the things we did because they were a well-prepared football team. But from that day on, with Woody at Ohio State and Bo at Michigan, the Ohio State-Michigan rivalry escalated to a new level.

Woody was depressed after that 1969 loss to Michigan. I really feel that a tiny doubt had been planted within Woody. Coach now believed that with Bo as coach, losing to Michigan every year was a possibility.

Woody's strategy? He'd outwork them, as always. We started talking on the way home from Michigan about what we had to do to win next year. Preparation for Michigan began when we arrived home. Bo became an obsession. We had to beat Michigan on the field and in recruiting.

We had a rug made and put the score on it so the players would have to walk on it all winter. We couldn't lose to Bo. That was the challenge. Woody was scared to death of Bo. He knew Bo was a good coach. He knew Bo's intensity level matched his. Woody considered Bo a threat because of Bo's insider knowledge of Woody and the Ohio State system. Woody predicted Bo would be the most successful coach in Michigan history. He was a keen observer of people and an unerring judge of ability. He pegged Bo correctly from the start.

**WE PRACTICED MORE FOR MICHIGAN** in the spring of 1970 than I had ever seen. I'd never seen so much intensity. As offensive coaches, we all started keeping manila folders with plays in them. By the end of spring practice, our folders were filled with Michigan plans.

During fall camp and two-a-day practices, we practiced for Michigan rather than our first three opponents. We didn't worry about any other opponent until the week of the first game. During the season, we'd practice those Michigan plays every Monday. When it was Northwestern week, we practiced for Michigan Monday, Tuesday, and Wednesday.

When Michigan week came in 1970, we had our game plan already put together. All we had to do was perfect it. Our 'Super Sophomores' were seniors now, and not one of them wanted to risk getting hurt so they wouldn't be able to play in 'The Game.'

So our practices that week weren't as sharp and crisp as they should have been. Everyone just wanted to get though practice because it was so very intense. But we weren't practicing as we well as we normally would have. We didn't look the way Woody wanted us to look. He'd get upset and walk off the field.

'I can't coach this team. You take over Earle. Run 'em a little bit!' So I'd get Rex in there and we'd call a couple plays and run 'em down the field and pretty soon, Woody would be sneaking back in to call the plays.

Thursday morning, the offensive coaches met at 8 a.m. As we walked into the meeting room, there was Coach Hayes was sitting in a chair, head bowed in his hands, arms rested on his spread knees. He sat there silently. We filed into the room and watched him, waiting for him to say something.

Finally, he said, 'We can't beat 'em.' He repeated it once or twice and then fell silent and never moved a muscle, with head in hand, his elbows resting on his knees.

Several of us said, 'Coach, they're not gonna beat us. No one's gonna beat our ass.'

**WE DIDN'T KNOW WHAT TO DO.** Woody stayed silent with his head bowed, both hands holding his chin, elbow on his knees, staring at the floor. Dead silence. *Deafening silence.* Finally, about 9:30, an hour and a half later, he mumbled, 'Maybe we ought to go robust. We can't get…we can't get humiliated.'

A couple of us would say, 'Oh, no, no, coach. We'll be OK. Our kids are gonna play.'

Then it was back to silence. Woody, staring at the floor, head in his hands, arms on his knees. He sat in that same position until about 11 a.m. Three full hours! We didn't know what to do. One by one, we finally got up and trickled out of the room to go get some coffee.

Woody was still in the room, sitting, staring at the floor, hands clasped on his chin, elbows resting on his knees.

As offensive coaches, we decided we had to get the Old Man up somehow. George Chaump, Rudy Hubbard, Ralph Staub, and I decided to give him a little talk.

'Coach, you've got to do something in the team meeting this afternoon. You've got to get the team's attention so they know you mean business. You're good at it. Why don't you take that plastic pitcher of water and heave it against the wall. It'll splatter, their eyes will damn near pop out of their heads. That'll get their attention!'

'You think I should do that?' Woody asked.

'Hey, only you can do that, Coach,' we said. 'It'd motivate this football team to no end.'

So we came in for our meeting and watched and waited to see what the Old Man had decided to do.

Finally, he came into the room. When the players fell silent, Woody exploded into a rage. He took that pitcher and threw it against the wall and delivered a talk and a half. We went out to practice Thursday, ran through plays Friday, and kicked their ass Saturday. I mean, we kicked their ass.

ON THE OPENING KICKOFF, Rich Ferko went down the field, hit their guy, and caused a fumble that we recovered on their 25-yard line. Little Rich Furko earned his scholarship right there. His move set the tone for the game. Our kids played like they were possessed. Leo Hayden ran the sprint draw through holes big enough for three trucks to drive through. The final score was 20-9. It could have been 40-9.

The dejected, morose Woody Hayes did a 360-degree turn after we won 20 to 9. In the locker room after the game, the first thing he did was take out a copy of a book Bo wrote about football. He held it in the air and yelled like Patton did to his troops, 'I read your book, you sonofabitch!'

Woody claimed Patton beat Rommel by reading his books. Now, Woody said he read Bo's football book about the sprint-draw.

Woody won and felt he knew everything, a complete personality change from the week of the game to after the game on Saturday. Dr. Jekyll and Mr. Hyde.

**WE WENT TO THE ROSE BOWL** in 1970 and lost to Stanford. We went from the I-formation to the Wishbone. Everyone was starting to run the Wishbone, beginning with Arkansas and Texas. We watched them play, and Woody thought that was a great-looking offense, that it looked more like his familiar Robust-T with the full-house backfield.

Woody was convinced we had the personnel to run it. He thought Rex could maybe run the ball better than he could pass, which I really didn't believe at all. We weren't exactly the masters of the passing attack, but it was solid enough to get us to the Rose Bowl. And the 1970 Rose Bowl game was one we should not have lost.

The night before the game, we went to the Monastery and some of our players partied quite a bit. The years 1969 and 1970 were bad years for drugs. Drugs were a fairly new wrinkle to all of the coaches. Without testing, it was hard to tell who was using. The players who were in deep were a bit easier to pick out, but the casual users were hard to detect, and we were just becoming aware of all the problems drugs brought to a team.

After the Rose Bowl of 1970, OSU coaching staffs from all the major university sports met at the golf course to hear several drug intervention folks talk. Some of the stories we heard that day were horrific. Some of the stories made me want to die. One point the counselors made clear: Marijuana was probably on campus to stay. As coaches, we would have to determine the level of player use that we would tolerate. This information session had the same effect on Fred Taylor, the basketball coach, and Woody. They were in disbelief. Woody walked out of the meeting.

In the 1971 season, we lost our last three games, to Northwestern, Michigan State, and Michigan. The Michigan game, where we lost 10-7, was the infamous sideline marker game in Ann Arbor. Woody knew the missed call ended our chance to win.

We lost the football, and they took over the game. I watched him charge after that sideline marker and heave it out on the field and thought, 'What the hell is he doing?' But when you think about it, he was telling the referees, you took the game away from us. That was pretty good thinking on the Old Man's part. He deflected all the attention away from losing the football game and turned it into a controversy about Woody Hayes and the down markers.

Calculated? Yeah, I think it was calculated. Pretty good thinking in my book. For all those times he had controlled himself after a bad call—this was the one time he let go. By God, he did it. God bless 'em. Obviously, he took the heat at Ohio State from the people running our program.

People started talking about getting rid of him. But thank God for Michigan's Athletic Director Don Canham, who stuck up for Woody. What would you expect with a rivalry so great as Bo and Woody?

Picture him charging down the sideline like a bull, short sleeve white shirt, black block 'O' cap, chin jutting out in disgust. That guy holding the sideline marker must have wondered what the hell was going on. Woody was charging at him, ripping the sideline marker from his hands, and throwing it out onto the field.

I recall how lucky I felt that season to have been part of the team and program. The dramatic end to the Michigan game even seemed like part of some grand plan. I'm glad I didn't know at the time it would be my last game at Ohio State.

After the 1970 season, I started paying a little bit of attention to head football coaching openings. Lou Holtz had already gone to William and Mary. An opening came up at North Carolina State, and Woody recommended me and Lou for the job. Lou got it. It was the first time I was recommended for a college head coaching job.

I also heard about other openings, including one at the University of Tampa. Eventually, Tampa would be my initiation into the fraternity of head coaching.

# Moving up

Tampa had a tradition of good hardnosed football. We had John Matuzek, who became the number one draft pick in the NFL in 1972. We had two tackles who were better than what we had at Ohio State. We had outstanding quarterbacks, Freddie Solomon

➲*Bowling: Tampa's offensive line that blocked its way into the Tangerine Bowl*

and Buddy Carter. They came to play football. It was

a team that reminded me of the kids at Massillon.

They loved to hit, and they loved to work. I agreed

to a three-year contract.

---

When the contract was finally written up, I noticed some potential problems. If I left before the contract was up, I'd have to pay back my moving expenses, and it specified my retirement wouldn't go into effect for three years from when I took the job. I never signed the contract because I wasn't going to agree to the terms. They weren't going to pay for the retirement plan. These stipulations were never discussed with me in the beginning. I went through the whole season without a signed contract. We started out 2 and 0, then went 2 and 2 and no one cared if I signed.

Then we beat Miami 7-0, and really clobbered Vanderbilt. We put some wins together no one thought possible, and we finished 10-2. After the season, the players voted to decline an invitation to the Tangerine Bowl. They didn't feel the Tangerine Bowl was good enough; they wanted to go to the Peach Bowl. They voted not to go at 3 o'clock in the afternoon. By that evening they had taken another vote, and we went to the Tangerine Bowl.

We played Don James' Kent State team, which had a guy I had never heard of at linebacker, named Jack Lambert. He made every tackle. He spent more time in our backfield than my quarterback. I told my center, 'You got to *block* that guy.' The center looked at me like I had just told him to lie down under a train.

We scored three touchdowns in the first half, and we never scored again. They scored eighteen points in the second half, and we hung on to win 21-18. But everybody knew who Jack Lambert was.

Suddenly, officials from the university's business office came to me with the revelation I'd never signed a contract. I said, 'I'm not signing any contract until the season is over and we get these other items resolved. I'm not going to pay back any money if I leave.'

About that time, Lou McCullough called from Iowa State and wanted me to fly to the Liberty Bowl to meet with him and his Iowa State administrators about a opening at Iowa State. I told Lou I wasn't really interested in Iowa State. Here I was in Tampa, sitting at 10 and 2, and I knew I could repeat that record next season. I knew after a third good year, I'd be able to go somewhere and get a top job. At that stage of my career, Iowa State was not a top job.

*Blatant Fowl:*
*Earle and his assistant chicken*

But Lou was adamant. He said they'd sneak me out of Tampa early in the morning and get me back before anyone knew I was gone. So I went to the Tampa Airport at five in the morning, waiting for my 6 a.m. flight, and in walks the biggest booster in Tampa athletics. He taps me on the shoulder, and gives me a stern look with eyes that could melt an ice cube.

'Where are you going?' he deadpanned, waiting to measure every word of my response.

It was as if he knew exactly what was going on. I didn't bat an eye and quickly responded, 'I'm going recruiting.'

'You're not going for a job, are ya? he shot back. 'We've lost three coaches in three years!'

Damn, I thought, this encounter will be all over town by lunch.

**I REALLY NEVER THOUGHT** I would take the Iowa State job. And in retrospect, I probably shouldn't have. The University of Tampa was paying me $20,000 yearly as head coach plus $2,200 for a television show. It was a big jump from the $14,000 salary as an Ohio State assistant, and I had coached in Tampa for one year before leaving for Iowa State. Tampa was a great football experience. We had great football players, and my proudest accomplishment is that almost every one of those athletes graduated. Tampa had a reputation for taking in renegades, but that wasn't really true. There are some very fine success stories from the University of Tampa.

When I officially accepted the job at Iowa, that same booster I saw at the airport had one final conversation with me.

'You weren't goin' recruiting, you sonofabitch,' he said.

'You're right,' I said. 'I wasn't. But I couldn't tell you that because I was just doing somebody a favor and going out for an interview.'

I took the job mostly because of Lou. One of my dearest friends in the world is Lou McCullough. He got me started as a college coach and was a great college coach in his own right. I would do anything for Lou and when he started his not-so-subtle arm-twisting, I couldn't resist. As far as I was concerned, Lou was one of the top athletic directors in the nation and I looked forward to working with him. The Iowa money was attractive, too. My first contract was for $25,000 with an additional $30,000 for a television program. And the deal was extra sweet because I loved the president at Iowa State, President Parks, a consummate straight-shooter and genuinely nice guy.

As athletic director, Lou was really adept at managing money and even better at raising it. One of Lou's most brilliant ideas was the Cyclone Club golf outing. We played golf, ate, and talked football. The outing season started in May and ended in August. By the time I was done talking football, I was worn out. But, boy, did it raise a lot of money for Lou and his athletic program. We all worked at getting people to donate to a new stadium, and when Lou ended his career at Iowa State, the athletic department was $2 million dollars in the black.

Iowa State didn't have any kind of reputation for winning at football and it was a tough job. We went 4-7, 4-7, and 4-7. I was damn near fired. I *would* have been fired if it hadn't been for Lou, the president, and a great Iowa State supporter, John Ruan, a trucking man from Des Moines who stood behind me and fought off the challengers for my job.

In the fourth season, we turned it around then went 8-3, 8-3, and 8-3, and played in the Peach Bowl and the Hall of Fame bowl games. It was the best record of any coach with my longevity at Iowa State.

Early on, it appeared as though we could always find ways to lose. We lost games we shouldn't have lost. Oklahoma State beat us 14-12 after we missed a chip shot field goal that would have won the game. Our guy had already kicked four field goals earlier in the game. We lost to Arkansas after they scored with twelve men on the field, a full wishbone with a flanker, and no official called it. We lost some very close football games in the early years.

**TO BE SUCCESSFUL AT IOWA STATE**, you had to win at least one of your key games every year—Colorado, Nebraska, Oklahoma. You had to win one of those and you had to be dominant against teams like Missouri, Kansas, Kansas State, and Oklahoma State. After my third 4 and 7 season, George Chaump and George Hill called me from Ohio State and said they wanted me to be their head coach at the Hula Bowl. Woody wouldn't go, and they wanted me. I was the only 4-7 football coach in America to ever be picked as head coach of the Hula Bowl in Hawaii.

I watched the players closely as we prepared for the Hula Bowl. The whole time I'm watching the workouts, I'm thinking, my kids at Iowa State are just as good, if not better than these guys here in Hawaii. I got a better quarterback, running back, tight end, defensive tackle. Why am I losing? I decided I needed to go back to Iowa State and work on building up the players' confidence.

So we began telling each player he was a little better than he thought he was. We built some team confidence, and we went 8 and 3. In 1976, we almost won it all. We beat Nebraska. We not only beat 'em, we stuck it to 'em pretty damn good.

Then we started to win. We won all five conference games, and we won three games outside the conference. As our recruiting improved, we won some more. The whole problem all along was attitude. It was a tremendous change.

I coached a 6' 6" offensive tackle at Iowa State by the name of Cunningham from Illinois. He was so big and so powerful, he could dominate you with a quick touch. Sometimes, people tried to take advantage of him. One night, Cunningham was challenged in a bar and decked a guy. His victim pressed charges and the prosecuting attorney believed if Cunningham plead guilty, the charge would be reduced to a misdemeanor and $100 fine. So we advised Cunningham to plead guilty. Damn if they didn't leave it a felony, charge him $100, and put it on his record. Now the guy has a record and any more fights could present a serious problem. He quickly got the reputation of a one-hit knockout artist. If you even mentioned the name—Cunningham—a one-punch bar fight scene came to mind.

ONE NIGHT I'M AT A PARTY and get a call from a local cocktail lounge. A voice on the phone says they just had an incident with Cunningham and the manager is really upset.

'How do you know it's Cunningham?' I asked. They replied they had identified him through one of the football programs. I promised to check it out. I called the dorm and spoke to his roommate. His roommate told me he left to go home to Chicago at three in the afternoon. Based on that departure there was no way he could be at that bar at 10 p.m. So I called his home in Chicago and he answered. I was relieved but increasingly furious at the bar owner. I called the bar back and spoke with the manager. 'If you EVER call me again and tell me Cunningham did something in your place and you don't know him from third base,' I said, 'I'll come down there and I'LL kick your ass.'

The bar owner was incredulous. 'You mean it wasn't your guy?'

I told him I just talked to Cunningham in Chicago. The bar owner said he didn't know how that could be. I told him *I* knew.

'If *anyone* is in a bar fight in this town,' I said, 'it's Cunningham. Cunningham *always* gets the blame.'

He said, 'Well, it might be.'

I said, 'What do you mean, it MIGHT be. That's the way it is. My player isn't even in town.'

Cunningham did have his moments though, and he persevered to turn it all around. He graduated, got a great job and family, and he wrote me a heartfelt letter thanking me for everything.

IN DECEMBER OF 1978, I was recruiting for Iowa State in the Miami area. Knowing Ohio State was playing in the Gator Bowl, I was trying to figure out how I might go see them. After talking with Ohio State assistant George Chaump I decided I would recruit right up to the time of the Gator Bowl and just drive up to Jacksonville to watch the Buckeyes.

In the heat of my Miami recruiting I finally looked at a map. For the first time, I realized how far away Jacksonville was from Miami. There was no way I could complete my recruiting and get to Jacksonville for the kickoff.

So I called George back with my regrets, finished my work, and watched the game from my Miami hotel room. I watched the whole game, right up until Art Schlichter threw that interception to Clemson's Charlie Bauman.

As soon as he intercepted the ball and began to run it back, I turned the television off and yelled, 'Sonofabitch—they lost the game!'

I walked down to my car to retrieve some extra Orange Bowl tickets, and when I returned to the room, I turned the television back on and heard the analysts saying, 'They ought to fire the guy immediately. He had no business hitting that player!'

I thought, what did I miss? Then the replays began. My first thought was, oh my God, Woody is gone. He won't be able to survive this.

The next morning I flew home to Ames. I called Jean to check in because the weather was worsening and I thought I might get stranded at O'Hare. She was the one who told me that Woody had been fired.

# Woody himself

Woody Hayes entered Ohio State history through two acts of God.

One was a hellacious snowstorm, the other a loss to Michigan. The snow started mounting on Thursday evening of game week. Although postponing the game was discussed, it wasn't a popular option.

⊃*Woody's sideline: The old football/drama coach displays his home-grown theatrics*

I was one of 40,000 there to witness the disaster.

Coach Wes Fesler's teams had played four straight

years against Michigan, in the rain. He compiled

a record of three losses and a tie. The 1950 Snow

Bowl did him in.

———————————

Since that time, of course, everyone claims to have been at that historic game. I actually *was* there. I was red-shirted on the OSU team, not yet eligible to play. I attended the game as a spectator. It was a near whiteout, and I arrived at the stadium just as Vic Janowicz kicked a field goal, which put OSU ahead, 3-2.

Michigan had taken the early lead on a blocked punt/safety. I was sitting in the west stands on the 40-yard line, right behind a little old lady wearing a huge snow-coated blanket. She had to be at least 80 years old and was watching that football game all alone. With 46 seconds left in the half, OSU hung grimly to their one-point lead, and it was third and nine, the ball deep in their own territory.

An Ohio State player by the name of Bob Demmel—a blocking wingback—entered the game. He was to replace our speedy wingback, Walt Klevay. When this little old lady saw Demmel enter the game, she noticed the change in strategy immediately. With 46 seconds to go, she threw off her blanket, jumped to her feet with snow flying everywhere, and yelled as loud as any woman I've ever heard.

'Don't punt the ball, Fesler!' she yelled into the blizzard. '*Please* don't punt the ball!'

Suddenly, I realized Ohio State could just hold onto the ball. Michigan couldn't move it. They hadn't moved it at all in the first half. The only play possible was a punt because the snow was so deep you couldn't stand up and move. Neither team could run or pass the ball. The kids were going through the motions of playing football because the weather was so bad.

The little old lady watched fearfully as the Buckeyes went into punt formation. A Michigan defensive tackle named Momson broke through, blocked the punt, and fell on it in the end zone for a touchdown. Michigan won the game, 9-3. I'll never forget that little old lady in the stadium. She was the first person in the stadium to know we shouldn't have punted. She knew disaster when she saw it.

That heartbreaking move ended Wes Fesler's career at Ohio State. I don't think he could ever accept the fact that the game continued despite the weather. No doubt, the contest should have been postponed. But the loss slammed the door shut on Fesler, and opened it for Woody. And from the day Woody arrived, OSU football would never be the same.

A FEW DAYS AFTER HE WAS HIRED, I went to the football office in the old physical education building and was introduced to him. Off the field, he was one of the most cordial, genuine people you would ever meet. He knew your name. He talked with you about all the important things, not the superficial topics. He remembered details about your family or your friends. His recall was remarkable. He was very direct in a conversation. He looked right at you and maintained eye contact. He had a gift for not just conversing but for absorbing the information you shared. There was never any doubt you had his attention. He was unique and personable.

On the football field, his personality transformed itself. Shortly after being hired, he called a series of practices inside the gym, just to observe the team's composition and potential. Everything went well enough through the opening drills.

When fall rolled around that first season, we saw a different side of

Woody Hayes. That's when the pressure started to mount. I remember the first time he threw his hat down and yelled, 'Shit, shit, shit, SHIT.'

Boy, that's when everybody took notice. The blood was flowing and the adrenaline was pumping. Guys who took their football seriously didn't want to attract his attention during practice. He was into it. He coached everything all over the field. He was into the offense, the defense, backs and quarterbacks, defensive ends. He was nothing like Coach Fesler.

If you ever did anything wrong under Fesler, he'd just come up to you and gently but firmly say, 'You can do better than that, son.' Woody didn't exactly say it that way. He'd throw that hat down, rip his shirt off, throw the whistle down, and yell a string of unprintable words.

The first time you witnessed his performance, you didn't know how to act. It was hard to take. We all laughed about it off the field, but most of the guys recognized the wisdom of avoiding his wrath. The fact that he showed such a genuine interest in each of us off the field helped make up for his demeanor on the field. If he made you miserable during practice, he always made a point of seeing you afterwards to smooth things over a bit.

**WHEN MY PLAYER STATUS ABRUPTLY CHANGED**, I was humbled by his integrity and example. When I was injured and the doctors said I couldn't play football again, I packed my gear and went home to Maryland. Woody sent an assistant coach after me. He said he expected me to come back, finish my education, and help coach football. In that day, an injury forfeited your scholarship. But because of Woody Hayes and his integrity, I was taken care of. He made sure I kept my aid and my chance for an education.

The impact of Woody was felt well into my early coaching career. My assistant position at Mansfield Senior High School was going well. By sheer coincidence, my wife, Jean, and I met up with Woody at a team picnic in May of 1955. The introduction was nothing out of the ordinary, just a pleasant exchange.

Months later, we were asked to attend an event and Woody happened to be there, too. He walked up, shook my wife's hand, and said 'Hi, Jean, how are you?'

She seemed a bit dazed, gave some reply, and the conversation was over. We were walking away, and I looked at her. 'What in the hell is the matter with you?' I said.

'He remembered my name,' she said. I told her he remembered *everyone's* name. 'No,' she said, 'no one remembers *my* name, but *he* remembered it.'

**WAS SHE IMPRESSED,** and it proved to be indelible. In 1966, I began at OSU as an assistant coach. For the first six years, I tried to never talk about the job at home. At that time, Jean and I had three little girls, Lynn, Michele, and Aimee. Our fourth, Noel, was born in 1974. I tried to make some time just to be a dad. When I came through the door, I would concentrate on kids and family. But once in awhile, I'd break my own rule and mention little incidents that would come to mind.

'You realize what Coach Hayes did tonight?' I said once. 'He picked up a projector and threw it against the wall.'

'Coach Hayes would never do that,' she said. 'You lie.'

Her answer stunned me. What an impression the guy made for my own wife to call me a liar. I didn't lie; he *did* throw the projector against the wall. But remembering her name made a great impression on her, and established his credibility forever.

As an assistant coach for Coach Hayes, your duties include recruiting, and my recruiting area was western Pennsylvania. I was hired July 1, 1966, to take over as the defensive backfield coach with Lou McCullough, the defensive coordinator. Because of the July 1 start date, I had missed all of spring recruiting and had to go out on the fall circuit.

While in the office one day, I was coming down the hallway, heading for the bathroom, and Coach Hayes passed me in the hall. He asked me how recruiting was and how many players I was going to get. I looked at him and told him I didn't know if I was going to get anybody. I explained that the competition over in western Pennsylvania was terrible. I explained that Michigan, Notre Dame, Pitt, and Penn State recruiters were swarming all over the place, and they were doing a good job. I'm just learning the ropes, I said.

He looked me in the eye and said I should be getting at least five to ten football players. I told him there was no way I could get five or ten, but I if I was lucky, I might get one. And that was just what I got—one.

**THE NEXT YEAR, MAKING THAT SAME TRIP** down the same hallway, I ran into Coach Hayes again. It was just before signing date, and he asked how I was doing with my recruiting and how many guys I was going to get. I told him I was doing better, and I was going to get between three and five. He told me I ought to get ten for sure and wanted to know what was the matter.

I told him I was going to get three for sure and they'd be three good ones. My recruiting efforts in western Pennsylvania were getting better because the coaches knew me and knew how I talked. I have that western Pennsylvania accent because I was born in Pittsburgh. If the local guys think you're from the valley, you're automatically in. Over there, I was in.

By the third year, I came walking down the same hallway and I was ready. I answered him before he asked me anything. 'I'm going to get ten, Coach,' I said. 'I'm going to get ten for sure.'

'You can't get ten,' he said. 'We can't take ten from western Pennsylvania. We're only going to be able to take 25 guys and you can't take ten!'

'I'm getting ten,' I said. 'You hear me.'

I just wanted to be sure he understood. Coach Hayes was a guy who perfected the art of applying pressure. If you couldn't take stress and pressure, you were miserable in his system. Oh, it was unbelievable how well he could stick you.

When you recruit for Coach Hayes, he stays with you for a solid week. Twenty-four hours a day. You go to the prospect's high school and meet the coach and principal. He talks to the kid at school, and then we make a home visit. You really work from about 7 or 8 a.m. until about 11 at night. If he was in someone's home, Coach Hayes never left before 11 p.m. He stayed and he sold, sold, sold.

He was the most dynamic guy in the kitchen you had ever seen. One of his big objectives was the kid's mother. He'd never leave a house until he had worked on the mother and sold her.

We'd visit the high schools all over western Pennsylvania. It was very hard to be with Coach Hayes because he was so quirky. He might slip off to sleep while you're talking to him. If you turn on the radio, he turns it off. If you wind up the window, he winds it down and you freeze your ass.

It was really difficult to be with him for such long periods. He would ask questions. The questions would turn into an interrogation and soon the driver's seat became the hot seat. You're under extreme pressure.

**WE WERE WORKING MY AREA** by car once, and I told him I had to stop at Greensburg Catholic High School to pick up film of an offensive lineman there. I asked if he wanted to just wait in the car while I picked up the film. He said, no, he would come in.

Jeez, when you went in a school with Coach Hayes, all the kids stare and everybody wants to talk to him. The principal, the superintendent, this guy, that guy, everybody wants a piece of him. I just wanted to run in and grab the film because I hadn't evaluated the guy yet.

The high school coach asked if we wanted to talk to the player, and Coach Hayes said, sure, he'd like to meet him. The kid was home sick, but the coach said he would call the house first so we could run over and see him.

I started to say no and Coach Hayes says, 'We're going.'

We go to this prospect's house. He's one of those tough-looking kids. He has the massive neck and the arms and the build of a football player. He looks the part, but I haven't looked at the films and have no proof he can play a lick.

We sit down and start talking to his dad. Notre Dame is in competition, but I know he's not qualified for Notre Dame. The kid needs more points on his entrance exams. I'm thinking, I may slip in here later after evaluating his film and get him.

Woody starts talking and all eyes are on him. I'm sitting in the corner of the room feeling aggravated. I'd wanted to look at films first to see if this guy was someone we wanted. All of the sudden Coach Hayes says, 'We want to offer you a scholarship.'

I can't believe my ears! I'm trying to give the signal to hold up. I'm trying to whisper to him that I haven't evaluated the kid yet. I'm starting to feel sweaty. He's having none of it. He's paying no attention to my frantic signaling and he offers him a full scholarship, room, board, and books. The kid and the dad are so impressed.

**I WALKED OUT OF THERE IN SHOCK.** I told him that I hadn't even looked at the film of the guy. I had no idea if he could play. I asked why he would offer him a scholarship. 'The kid had football in his eyes and football in his body,' he says. 'Don't worry about it, Earle.'

In the end, the kid chose Notre Dame and he did play a little football. Coach Hayes took a gamble on that kid without hesitation. He always trusted his instincts more than film.

This particular trip was winding down on a Thursday night. We were ready to fly back to Ohio State early Friday morning. As we headed to the airport, Coach Hayes wants to know where we were staying that night. I told him I had reserved a room for each of us at the Howard Johnson's across the street.

He told me no. He preferred that we stay in the airport for convenience. I told him I'd never stayed there and didn't know anything about it. He told me to get the rooms. I told him I already had the rooms held at the Howard Johnson's.

'Too bad,' Coach replied. 'Call our secretary and get us rooms in the airport.'

It must have been 10:30 that night when we finally got to the airport and returned the car. The airport was down to one available room. Now we're going to be roommates! There *were* two beds, thank God. So I go in there and think, oh God, this is really pressure.

I couldn't believe how the trip was going. Coach is the quirkiest guy. I turn the television on. He turns it off. He picks up a book and starts reading. So I figure I'll go into the bathroom. As soon as I get in there, he wants in the bathroom, too. The room seemed to be shrinking. He is everywhere.

Finally, he goes to bed and begins reading. I lay in bed, staring at the wall with the lights on. I'm thinking, how on earth am I going to get any sleep tonight. All of the sudden he puts his book down, reaches over, and turns out the light. He takes the covers, pulls them over his head, and he says, 'Fuck'em all.'

I think, oh my God.

As soon as the covers are over his eyes, he's asleep. He is snoring by the time the covers hit the top of his head. I lay awake and wonder all night who he was talking to. The next morning, I asked him what he meant with those last words before sleep.

'The alumni,' he said. He told me I had to put everything in the right perspective.

'Take their money,' he said, 'but you don't have to answer to those bastards for anything.'

I knew doggone well how he loved the alumni at Ohio State, so it wasn't a personal thing. But he did believe you had to keep them in their place. He felt the only way to preserve self-respect was to keep them from interfering. His little nightly anthem was the only way he could do it.

**OUR FOOTBALL RECORD AFFECTED MY HEART.** The better the season, the less tightness in my chest. My first year as an assistant was 1966 and we had a 5-4 season. In 1967, we were 6-3 and in 1968, we were undefeated, national champs. In 1966 I had an unbelievable tightness in my chest. Dr. Bob Murphy, the team physician, examined me. I told him I thought I had a problem and didn't know what it was.

'Well, join the club,' he said. I asked him what he meant.

'Every coach that comes in here under Coach Hayes has chest pains the first year,' he said. 'Adjust to it. Go home at night and take a Valium. Get into the bathtub every night to soak and cuss the Coach out.'

I took his advice a few times and my two little girls would be outside the door wondering who Daddy was talking to. I was talking to Coach Hayes, telling him all the problems I had, all the problems he had, and all the problems with football.

Dr. Bob's advice was on the money. Getting all that off my chest really helped. That was the psychology of coaching for Coach Hayes. You had to keep yourself in a mental state where you could deal with him. It took time to figure out a system that worked individually. But you had to find some kind of release, simply as self-preservation. It took time to get adjusted to Coach Hayes.

One of the legendary stories about Woody was how he would always ask one of the players to wash his back when he was in the shower. Players always hurried to get out of the shower so they wouldn't get stuck with Woody. He felt if you washed his back and then he washed your back, it would 'take the edge off.'

I think there's something to that concept, but I'm not sure exactly what. I never stayed around much to find out. Some psychologist somewhere must have told him that tactic, and he tried it.

**DURING MY FIRST YEAR OF COACHING**, I was asked to be the coach down on the field. It wasn't a prestige position. The other coaches didn't want the detail. Esco Sarkkinen wasn't there for the games, he was out scouting. Upstairs in the box were Bill Mallory and Lou McCullough. I recall playing Minnesota at their place, and they jumped out to a 14-0 lead. Minnesota coach Maury Warmath was a good one and, finally, in the fourth quarter, we score and make it 14-7.

I'm on the sideline calling the defenses and communicating with the defensive team. After they score, Woody approaches me. 'Get the Kangaroo team ready,' he said. That was our code for the onside kick. There's over 14 minutes to go in the ball game, and the score is 14-7. But I wasn't sure the old clock in the stadium was accurate. No one was sure of the time on that ancient clock. Anyway, he told me to get the Kangaroo ready and looked at me.

At the same time, Lou McCullough is telling me over the headphones to get away from Coach Hayes because they don't *want* the Kangaroo team.

Instead of saying, 'Okay, Coach,' I started to move away from him. All the sudden, he hit me in the back and said, 'I said get the Kangaroo.'

'Screw it, you guys,' I said into the headphones, 'he's getting the Kangaroo team whether you want it or not.'

I couldn't have this going on. McCullough is screaming in my ears from up top—'NO KANGAROO!!!!'—and Coach Hayes is waiting for it. He was the head football coach, and if he says the Kangaroo, we do the Kangaroo.

So we do the Kangaroo, they recover it, go down and kick a field goal, and they beat us 17-7. You should have seen what happened in that locker room after that game. There were five or six coaches over on one side and here comes Coach Hayes. He comes in there and we're watching him around the corner.

**THIS IS THE OLD MINNESOTA STADIUM**, a dingy old locker room with some kind of plyboard dividers in it. Coach Hayes takes his left fist and puts it right through that plyboard divider, making a big hole in it. Holy mud, I couldn't believe he put his fist right through there. I didn't see him grab his hand or move his knuckles afterwards. It was like he felt no pain.

The funny part about the whole incident was that it became somewhat legendary. The next time we go up there to play, all the players were standing around the hole saying, 'This is it! There's where he did it,' trying to recreate the whole scene. I'm here to tell you he hit that board with a vengeance. It was pure emotion that sent his fist through that thing.

Anyone who appreciates good acting would have appreciated Coach

Hayes. He was the greatest of actors. It was always said that Woody took a razor blade to his hat before he threw one of his infamous hat-ripping tirades. I never saw him do any of that, although the story around the locker room was that one of the assistant trainers 'prepared' his hat and made sure he had a bunch of those cheap, five-'n-dime watches, so Coach Hayes would be ready for any tantrum.

He got your attention and you played hard in practice because of his dramatics. 'Oh, Jesus, look at that,' you thought. Or, 'Look what he's doing to so-and-so.'

You didn't want any of the theatrics directed at you. Being an actor was very important to Coach Hayes' success. He once said he learned about acting from his father. His father was an educator—a principal and then a superintendent in Newcomerstown. Woody said his Dad was the best actor he'd ever seen.

Coach Hayes instilled the importance of discipline into my soul. As a coach, I chose not to go about it quite the same way he did. You could make a mistake on the football field with Woody and be okay. But if you were on the problem list for off-the-field behavior, things would be twice as ugly. If a kid skipped class or got into trouble on High Street and Woody found out about it, the wrath of God would descend.

**HE'D GIVE THE OFFENDER** a little extra shot. It might be physical sometimes, but it wasn't anything that could hurt you. It looked worse to the team, and that was the effect he wanted. He never hit anybody to hurt them. It was just an attention-getter. Once, Woody greeted one of his truly great players in his office—you always knew you were in trouble if he called you in the office—by grabbing him by the throat. Then he threw the player down, put his foot on his throat, and said, 'Now don't lie to me.'

My bet is it's pretty hard to tell a lie in that position. The whole scene was a strange kind of compliment actually. Woody didn't carry on like that unless he cared for you.

He had great personal heroes like Ralph Waldo Emerson, General

George Patton, and a German submarine commander named Karl Doenitz. Woody was a German submarine freak. He always felt Germany could have won the war if they had used submarine warfare, and he was intrigued with the whole concept. Coach Hayes quoted those military guys as his heroes. He adopted the philosophy of Ralph Waldo Emerson, believing that praise was not a constructive activity, but instead it actually destroyed you.

He used that philosophy during an unforgettable speech following the Rose Bowl win in 1969, capping off our winning season in 1968. As a program, we were on a high. We had beat Southern California and were National Champions. Woody needed to meet with us before he left for Vietnam as part of the group entertaining the troops. I don't think I'd ever seen my fellow assistants—Bill Mallory, Lou Holtz, George Chaump, Lou McCullough, or Esco Sarkkinen—so proud. We had just won the National Championship.

**OUR SUSPENDERS WERE BURSTING**, and we were thinking we had done such a great job. Woody called us in at 10 a.m. He had an announcement.

'Well,' he said, 'I think I can get you coaches the same contract next year as you had this year, no problem.'

Here, we were thinking we would get a big raise. There was Woody saying he would get us the same contract. We weren't making very much money anyway, so a raise would have been nice. Then he added, 'If any of you son-of-a bitches are thinking about leaving me, you better tell me now, because I don't want to read in the paper that I'm losing a football coach. It won't go down easy with me if you're leaving and don't tell me. And if any of you *are* leaving, I already have your replacement for next year. I've talked with him and he is ready to come.'

Here we were surrounded with accolades. The alumni are patting us on the back, and Woody took the air right out of our sails. He purposely sent us back to Earth real quick. All this because Emerson said praise weakens you.

Woody wasn't about to heap any praise upon us and say we did a good job. That wasn't his way. It wasn't that he didn't take pride in the season. He just wanted us to keep our heads on straight and keep us humble.

THE ONLY TIME I HEARD ANY PRAISE FROM WOODY was when I was leaving in 1972. I had been at OSU for six years as an assistant. I went in to talk to him and announced I had accepted a job at the University of Tampa.

He looked at me and said, 'Earle, you never know when I'm going to retire.'

I said, 'Coach, you're going to be coaching this football team for ever and ever, and you're going to die on the 50-yard line, so don't talk to me about that.'

He told me I shouldn't go to the University of Tampa because it had a renegade reputation. I told him I was 41 years old and Tampa was the only one who wanted me. 'Besides,' I said, 'they have some good football players and I can win there.'

Every year during the six years I was an OSU assistant, Coach Hayes had one coach selected for his doghouse. That lucky guy would be given special care; Woody would make life a little bit different for that particular coach. During staff meetings at the beginning of every year, Woody would choose a young coach to pick on.

The National Championship year, 1968, was my year in the box. As an offensive coach, you always work closer with Coach Hayes, much more than as a defensive coach. In 1968, right after the national title, it was my year to be Woody's guy. I got hell about everything and could do nothing right. I coached guards and centers, some with great talent, but it didn't matter.

Spring practice is in April, and before the national title year we had a closed scrimmage for parents. Only parents and families could attend. Coach Hayes decided that following the intersquad game he would introduce each position and have each coach step up to the microphone.

The defensive backs were with Lou Holtz; the quarterbacks with George Chaump, the defensive ends were with Sark, and then he came to me with offensive guards and centers.

When it came my turn, there was a big pause. He couldn't think of my name. I could hear Anne Hayes in the front row, yelling 'Earle Bruce! Earle Bruce!'

**JEEZ, I THOUGHT, AM I IN BAD TROUBLE HERE.** Now Woody remembered everyone's name he'd ever met. The greatest insult you could get from Woody was for him to forget your name.

I knew it was going to be hell and I was right. I got to the point where I would have taken a job flipping hamburgers, that's how bad it was. And Woody's persecution wasn't just relegated to coaching. Off the field, he'd ask me about a particular student and a particular class.

I'd start backtracking and covering my ass. Oh, God, as an assistant did you have to cover your ass. You never wanted to say, 'I don't know.' You had to come into those coaches meetings knowing what your kids were doing in every class, including how many classes they had missed and what their grade point was to the tenth.

Coach Bill Mallory was in charge of the weather. One day it was raining and Coach Hayes asked Mallory for the weather forecast. He didn't know the weather and said, 'I'll be right with you, Coach.'

Off he ran to call the weather bureau for the latest forecast. Woody would say, 'Goddamn it, I can do that! You bring that forecast in here with you and you better know exactly what it is when you come in that door.'

So every morning Mallory would have the weather written out so we'd know whether to cover the field for practice or cover the stadium field before a game. If you failed any of your jobs, boy, would you hear it from Coach Hayes. And if you were the designated man 'in the barrel,' like I was in 1968, you didn't want any additional infractions adding to your agony.

There was never any reason why a particular person was chosen for a turn in the barrel. It just was your designated time to pay your dues. When Coach Hayes was picking on you, your life was a living hell. Every day of 1968, all day long, was my year of hell. And after awhile, you started to take it personally. The absolute worst was forgetting my name in front of all the players, coaches, and parents during the spring practice. But by then, the damage was done.

**ONE OF MY GREATEST AWAKENINGS** came during spring practice in a drill we used to call 'half-line.' The center, guard, tackle, tight end, full backfield, and the quarterback run plays to the right side. Then we switch and run plays to the left side.

One day, he said, 'You come with me, Earle.' We get a graduate assistant and another coach and we prepare for the drill. I start coaching the offensive line, giving direction for the half-line drill, and we run a play.

I thought fullback Jim Otis hit the wrong hole. When the players return from the play, I start getting after Otis. The Old Man looks at me with his black ball cap pulled way down. He squints his eyes together so you can hardly see his eyeballs and he says, 'You get over there and take care of the defense. *I'll* coach the offense.'

What a mistake on my part! I broke an unwritten rule by talking to the fullback. I could talk to a guard or a tackle, but I better never talk to a fullback. The offensive players were Woody's domain and they never made mistakes when he was coaching. So he put me over on defense to work the half-line.

He was a control freak. And, of course, the kids picked up on it. I would tell my players, 'Don't say anything, or I'll work your ass a little harder.' Even when I was 'in the barrel', I always had a great relationship with my players. Woody's tirades would actually bind us together.

Because it was my turn in the barrel, my kids were under his constant scrutiny, and they suffered along with me. Sometimes it seemed Woody was way out there in his own universe and we were all together on the other side. That feeling wasn't all bad. The loyalty was always for Woody.

But we all worked together to show him, to win his approval.

He treated me like a goddamn dog in 1968, but somehow we all made it through. Months later, Woody singled out another coach in a staff meeting to pick on. I sat in my chair and cheered inside. My time in the box was over.

I'VE SEEN HIM FIRE ASSISTANT COACHES on the spot. He fired George Chaump twenty times. If you read Bo's book, you'll read where he fired Bo about fifteen times. He never really fired me, but he fired me from some of the internal team jobs I'd been assigned.

The worst assignment was picking the team movie every Friday night. I had to pick the team movies for Friday night, and once in Minnesota we had a problem. Normally, I would just go buy the paper and give it to him. He'd say, 'We'll go to this certain movie because it starts at 7:30.'

Then we'd be back in our hotel rooms by 10 p.m. and early to bed for Saturday's game. But on that particular night in Minnesota, I'm sitting there with my players having dinner, looking over the paper's movie schedule. There's only two movies starting at 7:30. One is a Walt Disney movie, and the other was some movie called *Easy Rider*.

I didn't know anything about *Easy Rider*, but the players told me that if I made them go see a Disney movie, they'd throw me in the lake behind the hotel. They said they weren't going to see any more Walt Disney movies.

So I talked with Coach Hayes about the movie. He asks which movie we should go see and I told him what the players said about throwing me in the lake. I suggested no Disney movie. He asked about the other movie, *Easy Rider*. He asked what I knew about it. 'Absolutely nothing,' I said. 'I never heard of it. I don't get to go to any movies, Coach. I haven't been to a movie in two years.'

'Okay,' he said. 'Go to *Easy Rider*. So we took the kids to the movie. I quickly learned the plot involved drugs, motorcycles, and explosions. I never did really understand what the point of that movie was. I had never even heard of some of the stuff in that movie. We get back at 9:45 and assistant coach Dave McClain—'Little Scooter' we used to call him, because he was always in such a hurry— gets off the first bus immediately. There's Woody waiting.

'How was the movie, fellas?' Woody asked.

'It's the worst movie I've ever seen,' Coach McClain said to Coach Hayes.

Woody wanted to know what was wrong with it and Dave told him it was about drugs and shooting people. I knew I had just been stabbed in the back! Scooter got me real good. The *Easy Rider* experience would be one that would haunt me. That season we had been averaging about 40 points a game. But the next day against Minnesota, the victory only netted 30 points.

The following Monday, Woody said, 'You know, teams either get worse or teams get better. We're getting worse. *Why* are we getting worse?'

Well, the real answer to Woody's question was our failure to stop their slip-screen pass all day. However, Woody's analysis of our performance narrowed down to one thing: the team viewing of *Easy Rider*. Being an offensive coach, I couldn't critique our defensive flaws with the slip-screen pass, so I just sat there.

**WHEN WOODY BLAMED** the team's performance on the movie, I could feel my ass get tight. He then launched into a tirade about the movie and how bad it was and how the team played like the movie. Finally he says, 'Who's in charge of the movie?'

I replied, 'I am.'

He looks up and said, 'You're fired. Rudy Hubbard, you're in charge of the movies from now on.'

Thank God, I thought. I'm fired. Was I ever glad to be rid of that headache. Unfortunately, the same thing happened when I was in charge of the music, too. He fired me from that detail. He objected to what we were playing in the locker room. I said, 'I just put on what the players bring in.'

'We can't have that,' he said. 'Where's Rudy!'

So I lost two jobs to assistant coach Rudy Hubbard. Rudy would often say to me, 'I don't want any more of your jobs. Why don't you start doing 'em right?'

**GETTING COMFORTABLE WITH COACH HAYES** was never a good idea. He asked me once during the Michigan game if I'd put my job on the line for a play I wanted him to run. It was the 1969 Michigan game; we had a third and 9.

We had a pass play called, '98-Gold', which was a post pattern over the middle to Jankowski. It was a type of a flood pattern and they took their safety man, Betts, and ran him to the flat, which left the post pattern open.

That was not the normal Michigan-style coverage, but they got into it somehow. I could see it would work from up in the press box, and I said 'Let's run 98-Gold.'

Woody listened and said, 'You think that'll work?'

I said, 'Yes, Coach—98-Gold—it's good.'

'Would you bet your job on it?' he said.

I was shocked and it took a couple of seconds for me to swallow hard and finally say, 'Yeah, YEAH, YEAH, I'll bet my job on it—98-gold.'

And 98-Gold went for a touchdown! I thought we could have scored about three more times on that play, but once it got to be 20-9 the Old Man kept that ball on the ground the rest of the afternoon.

Coach Hayes felt if you're ready to pound the table and be adamant in your conviction of choosing the right play, then he'd be willing to listen to you. But if you were just a milk-toast kind of guy and he challenged to bet your job on a play, you better be willing to do just that.

You didn't say, 'Oh, no, Coach. No.' Then you didn't get any plays called. You had to be forceful and positive to make it with Woody. You had to have courage to go into his office or demand a play to be called. But if you were wrong, he wasn't one to hold a grudge. I think he always admired individual tenacity and the desire to have your opinion heard.

He always asked you to write a critique at the end of the season. One or two years down the road, some of the suggestions I'd offered were reborn as his new ideas. I took it as a compliment, because it showed his acceptance of my ideas. George Chaump saw his ideas used when he joined the staff. Ohio State went from a fullback off-tackle to tailback off-tackle to feature the talents of a young guy named Archie Griffin. You can't believe what a sales job he had to pitch. Coach wasn't one to change his mind without a great deal of thought.

**WOODY LIVED IN MY SUBCONSCIOUS.** I frequently had this nightmare that I'd be sitting on top of the practice facility when Woody came into work at six in the morning to look at film. In my dream, I'd drop a concrete block on his head. Oh, my God, I had that dream over and over and over again. I remember his wife, Anne, was once asked if she'd ever considered divorcing him. 'Divorce, no,' she said. 'Murder, yes.' I knew what she meant.

In the 1971 Michigan game, Coach Hayes lost control. The action that triggered the whole spectacle was when the defensive back from Michigan, Thom Darden, came through the line and fouled our receiver, Dick Wakefield.

When that foul wasn't called, Coach Hayes went berserk on the sidelines. The call was a critical one because it prevented a chance for us to score. It was actually offensive pass interference, and we lost the game 10 to 7.

If the pass interference call had stuck, we might have scored. The missed call meant we had now lost three games in a row, Northwestern 14-10, Michigan State 17-10, and now Michigan 10-7. Woody began with a down marker and threw it out on the football field. Then he started to tear up the chains. He picked up more down markers and threw them at a back judge. From my position in the press box, I was truly unable to comprehend what was happening. He was in frenzy.

There was talk after that incident that he might have embarrassed the University and there was talk of dismissing him. I was just an assistant coach and didn't know much about these things, but I didn't think they'd act. The guy who really saved Coach Hayes' butt was Don Canham, the athletic director from Michigan.

He made a big public statement about how the incident was unfortunate, but you should expect something like that in a situation as combative as the Ohio State/Michigan game. Woody Hayes and Bo Schembechler had made this rivalry so fierce that you have to expect something like this to happen. No one should lose his job over something like that.

At the time, I thought it was bad example for a coach to perform like that. I also knew that as a head football coach, it's difficult to keep everything in perspective. When some guy takes the game away from you and your team because of a bad call, he can go on with his work. But you have to face that one split-second decision all year.

It was a bad call, and all the broadcasters knew it, too. Everyone agreed the official made a terrible call. Coach Hayes reacted by grabbing that sideline marker and heaving it on the field. You should have seen the faces of those guys holding the chains.

We assistant coaches got that piece of film cut down and put it on a clip to watch again and again when he was gone from the office. It was unbelievable to watch the whole scene unfold. It was a spontaneous act, not a malicious one. We laughed like hell every time we looked at it. We weren't laughing at him, we were laughing at the incident.

What a great actor! He was worthy of an Oscar. The attention it received did help take a little bit of the heat from the loss itself. Woody's raw emotion excited people and made them say, 'Oh, my God, that was something.'

It was his nature to let his emotions flow. His passion for everything is what set him apart.

# Replacing the master I felt

an emptiness in my heart because I knew

that it wasn't Coach Hayes on the sidelines of the 1978

Gator Bowl. As I watched, I knew he was sick. He had

suffered a lot of mood swings because of his diabetes.

To this day, I'm convinced he was in a diabetic stupor.

ↄ*Changing of the guard: the pupil takes over the classroom*

He was a time bomb ready to explode. I really don't think he knew he hit that kid. Everyone in college football was in shock. No one knew how to react. We were hoping that what we saw hadn't happened, and yet it had.

———————

How many people knew that after all this calmed down, Woody flew to Charley Bauman's house and spent a day of his life with that kid? He never said he was sorry, but Woody told him by being there that he didn't like what had happened. He called the coach, set it up, and tried to make things right with Charley Bauman.

Right after Woody was fired, the talk started about who was going to replace Woody Hayes. And the guy discussed most was Lou Holtz. I laughed. Holtz was making $350,000 at Arkansas and Woody made $44,000. But the Holtz speculation continued.

It took a while, but my phone began ringing. The story was that Woody was asked to resign. First he said yes, then he changed his mind and said, 'No, Goddamn it, you fire me if you want to get rid of me. I'm not going to resign.'

I don't think anybody really wanted to fire him, but the media frenzy was too great for the president of the university to ignore. Woody had already been talking with his assistants about his eventual retirement. But he was concerned about what would happen to the assistants and he never could make a firm decision about leaving.

The consensus among his friends was that Woody shouldn't have been fired. The better decision would have been to move him into another position within the athletic department. They finally did that some years later when they named him 'Football Coach-Emeritus', and gave him an office in the ROTC building.

When I first started thinking about the Ohio State job, I wondered if I should express an interest. Or wait for someone to call me. I decided to call Athletic Director Hugh Hindman, just to tell him that I was interested. I told him that if candidates from the 'outside' were to be considered, I'd like to be put on the list. Hugh said he appreciated the call and they'd get back to me. He was very businesslike, with no promises.

I went along with my normal business. I stayed active in recruiting for Iowa State and kept my lines of communication open with friends back in Columbus. A newspaper ran a story mentioning the top five or six candidates. My name was included, so I felt I might be seriously considered.

**WITHIN A COUPLE OF WEEKS THE PHONE RANG.** Hugh Hindman called and told me Ohio State would be interviewing during the annual coaches convention in San Francisco, and I was asked to prepare for an interview. The other candidates were longtime Woody assistants George Chaump and George Hill, along with Don James from the University of Washington, Ron Meyer at SMU, and Rudy Hubbard.

Don James withdrew his name after Washington gave him a $100,000 raise to stay. Holtz was not a top contender because of the money. Ohio State was viewed as a top ten position to the public, but in the coaching profession it was one of the 'poverty' jobs, thanks to Woody. He never wanted much money, and he kept all the other salaries in line with his. So I felt if I went to the convention and sold myself well I had a chance.

I remember flying into San Francisco. I was not too consumed with the upcoming interview because I had a great job. We were coming off an 8-3 regular season and we had great kids coming back. I loved Ohio State, but I wasn't sure I wanted to return to Columbus and give up everything I had worked for at Iowa State.

Several things weighed on my mind. Ohio State's facilities weren't very good at that time because Coach Hayes had never worried about that aspect. It would take some work to get the facilities improved enough to use as a tool in recruiting kids. Another item to contend with was simply following Coach Hayes. A lot of coaches wouldn't want those shoes to fill. Money was a consideration.

Another concern was the reputation that Ohio State and Columbus was 'the graveyard of coaches.' The average coach would be tentative about Ohio State because of that label. Coach Hayes was fired for losing to Michigan three years in a row. The Charley Bauman/Clemson incident didn't help, but Coach Hayes' unpopularity was enhanced by three straight losses to Michigan. Yet after all this, I still felt strongly about my school and knew if it was offered, I'd probably take the job.

**I DID PRETTY WELL AT THE INTERVIEW.** I talked about recruiting, my philosophy of football, and assistant coaches. My record helped further my cause. I had compiled a record of 82-12-3 in high school coaching. I was at Ohio State when the Buckeyes won the national title in 1968. I was 10 and 2 at the University of Tampa in my first head coaching job, and I took Iowa State to a bowl game with the best record in school history over a six-year period. No one else being considered had accomplished that. No one had the background I had in coaching, so it was just a question of me faring well during the interview process.

The only question I was asked was whether I would ever embarrass the university. Hugh Hindman told me confidentially after the interview that I was the guy, and the selection would happen within the next day. He said they wanted to name their new football coach before the end of the convention. So I waited around, listening to everyone and trying to learn as much as I could. The media always think they can name the guy. I was standing around with a bunch of guys in the lobby of the hotel and Dick Otte, the former *Dispatch* sports editor was standing around telling this group of guys who was going to get the job. He never mentioned

Earle Bruce and I had just been told the job was mine.

I returned to Ames. Hugh called and asked if I would accept the job, and I quickly said yes. He asked that I not say anything to anyone until I heard back from him. I agreed to keep quiet, but I knew the word would spread without me.

Not more than a few minutes passed before the phone calls started coming. It was like the phone was tapped. I'm sure Hugh had to tell someone. Before you knew it, I was inundated with phone calls from Iowa to Ohio. I asked Jean to answer the phone and tell everyone I wasn't available. I told Lou McCullough I'd accepted the job and he was so happy for me. He let me know if it was any other school making me an offer, Iowa State would fight like hell to keep me. But, he said, he'd never stand in my way of returning to Ohio State.

**LEAVING IOWA WAS TOUGH**, because I had many emotional ties. Our program was becoming big time football, and we were getting the big time players, too. The program was accepted and recognized on its own merits. The most emotional moment was saying farewell to the team. I met them at training table and there were tears all around. These were *my* kids. I had been there six years and many of these kids had been around for most of those years. I think they would have resented it if I left for any other school, but they understood and shared my happiness because I was going back to my alma mater.

Even the lady who ran the training table cried. She didn't like me when I first started because I was too much of a disciplinarian. But as the program turned around she fell in love with our system and the players. I wrapped up recruiting for Iowa State by visiting one of the top prospects in the state. His mother had heard on television that I was supposed to go to Ohio State.

'You're not going to even be at the school' she said. 'You're going to Ohio State. You won't even be here next year!'

'No, I won't,' I said. 'I am going to Ohio State. But your son belongs at Iowa State, no matter who the coach is. I gave six years of my life to

Iowa State, and I came here to make sure your son was still interested. I wouldn't think of pushing him or the program aside.'

She thanked me for my honesty, and I did feel very loyal to Iowa State and I was appreciative of the opportunity the school had provided for me. The kid did wind up at Iowa State and was a starter.

**THE NEXT DAY, THE OSU BOARD OF TRUSTEES** approved my hiring. I flew to Columbus for the formal announcement. I went to President Harold Enarson's house for dinner. I remember athletic director Hugh Hindman telling me at one point I had a phone call. It was Woody. 'Congratulations, Earle!' he said. I was struck by how upbeat he sounded. All the weight of the world had been lifted from his shoulders.

I told him thanks and I knew it would be a tough job following in his footsteps. 'I know it's not going to be easy, Coach' I said. 'You've done a hell of a job here.'

He said he was happy that I'd been chosen and he would be there for me whenever I needed support. We talked for about ten minutes. As I hung up the phone, I knew he'd keep his word and be there for me, no matter what. To this day, I have no idea who called Woody to tell him I was at the President's house. I just know it was a gracious gesture and gave me a great feeling about coming to Ohio State.

I spent the night at the President's house and Hugh picked me up early the next morning. We went to breakfast and the 11 a.m. news conference at the Fawcett Center. I was given a new scarlet and gray tie to wear, and Hugh introduced me as the new head football coach. I talked about how much I was looking forward to the challenge and acknowledged how difficult it would be following Coach Hayes.

Everything went perfectly, or so I thought. But before the ink could dry on the contract, my appointment was being challenged by the NAACP. The leader of the Columbus chapter was upset because Rudy Hubbard, a former black assistant coach and a coach at Florida A & M, was passed over for the job.

The head of the NAACP actually asked me about it as part of my news conference. I simply listened to him make his point and said, 'Next question.' That was all I could do. I wasn't prepared to deal with that. This group was upset about Rudy, and I couldn't respond to that. Rudy, being the good friend that he is, said he didn't feel discriminated against. Instead, he wished me well.

It had been a grueling day. I fired six of Woody's assistants. I knew all of them, but I had to have my own people. The last guy I was to interview was Bill Myles. I greeted him outside my new office in the narrow clutter-filled hallway that surrounded the core of St. John Arena.

'Bill,' I said, 'I'm finished for today. If I have to go back in my office for one more interview tonight, you don't have a job. Maybe tomorrow morning I'll feel a little fresher. Let's meet at 8 in the morning.'

Since I had just fired six assistants, including Alex Gibbs and George Hill, Bill was thrilled at the prospects of coming back tomorrow. He was happy to have escaped being a seventh casualty.

I shouldn't have been placed in a position where I had to fire Woody's assistants. Everyone knew I was going to bring as many of my assistants as would come, but athletic director Hugh Hindman asked me to at least give Woody's assistants an interview, talk to 'em and give 'em an opportunity.

I DID KEEP SEVERAL OF WOODY'S ASSISTANTS—George Chaump, Glen Mason, and Bill Myles. Chaump didn't last but two days before he decided he wanted to go to Tampa. I tried to talk him into staying, but he was a little hurt at being passed over for the head coaching job and thought the time was right to move on.

To replace Chaump, I hired Fred Zeckman, Art Schlichter's high school football coach from Washington Court House, who used to work for Bob McNea, one of my mentors, who I hired as my recruiting coordinator. I wanted to make a statement to the high school coaches in Ohio about how important I thought it was to have a high school coach be represented on my staff.

Without catching a breath, it was time to hit the road and start recruiting. The first speech I made in Ohio as head football coach was in Marietta. There were two kids there already committed to Ohio State, and I went back to recruit a center named Brown. Glen Cobb followed, then Tim Spencer and Marcus Marek. Cobb said he was going to Penn State but I convinced him to become a Buckeye.

**OUR FIRST RECRUITING CLASS WAS DAMN GOOD.** It was an impressive bunch of kids. Then I studied film of the last several Michigan games, which showed they were running an option play that had no chance of success. I like to have died! Where in the hell's the option? There was no option there. They had run it twelve times during the course of the ball game.

If you were Michigan you'd be lickin' your chops. Michigan must have wished Coach Hayes would never leave.

'Jesus Christ,' I said. 'This isn't Coach Hayes' football. Who in the hell was running this attack?'

I vowed to change things. We worked hard starting in the off season. The team had never done much in the off season. I kept all the coaches in, and we worked all summer. The coaches said they had never worked so hard. We had mandatory Saturday workouts and when a couple of guys didn't show, I'd send assistant coaches to go after them.

I'd run them extra, make them work after practice, whatever. After a few days of extra running, they started to get the message. There was no getting away with anything. The kids had to know this was a commitment and they'd better be there.

As we approached camp in August of 1979, I didn't know what to expect. We were going to have a lot of fifth-year seniors, although they lacked a lot of starting time. But they had speed, and speed probably saved us.

When we looked at films of the offensive line, they weren't coming off the ball. But as the season went on, they kept improving. They just kept getting better and better. Guards Ken Fritz and Mike D'Andrea were

⊃*The Head Buck: Earle takes over the sidelines*

good football players. Center Tom Waugh, tackle Tim Burke, and tackle-tight end Bill Jaco came into their own. Before the season, we were picked fifth in the league. Michigan State was picked number one. A lot of fans were apprehensive. I was the new kid on the block.

It seemed like I was speaking to groups every breakfast, lunch, and dinner. I was all over the state, speaking to every group possible. Imagine my surprise when one day at practice, Todd Bell, one of our great players from Middletown, asked me, 'Who's our head coach? Have you seen him? He's never here.'

I thought, damn! I've been away too much doing all these speeches. It was eye-opening to have one of my players tell me I hadn't been spending enough time with the team. They wanted a football coach who was around! And from that point on, I made sure my players came first.

I always kept an open door policy. If you wanted to talk, you came to me. If I don't see you, then I'll send for you. At the end of every quarter, I'd sit down with each player individually and see how they were doing. If they were not playing, I wanted them to tell *me* why. We talked about academic problems, football problems, problems with life off the field, girlfriends, drugs, alcohol. I tried to always be there for them.

**AFTER THE WHIRLWIND SPEAKING TOURS** came to an abrupt halt, it was time for football. The 1979 season started with a big win over Syracuse, then a tough win on the road at Minnesota. My defensive secondary coach, Pete Carroll, told me at halftime, 'You're on your own, Coach. I'm out of answers.'

They were using a run and shoot offense and we couldn't stop the trap play, or other basic, simple plays. And we had key guys knocked out. Defensive back Vince Skillings was knocked out. Our left tackle, Tim Burke, fell and separated his shoulder on Friday before the game.

We were playing guys out of position but we finally start to come back in the second half. Art Schlichter finally starts to mix the run and the pass, and Jerome Foster blocked a field goal, which resulted in one hell of a comeback, 21-17.

Some of our players and staff told me privately after the game, 'You know, Woody couldn't have done that. Woody wasn't very good when he got behind on the road, especially in the Big Ten.' Who knows? Woody didn't often have to come back. But we won in Minnesota, beat Washington State at home, and that set up a huge game at UCLA.

Trailing again, we came back in the two-minute drill to win 17-13. It's one thing to practice the two-minute drill well. It's another thing to execute it in a game. After we took off from the Los Angeles airport to fly home, the American Airlines pilot flew us over the Rose Bowl in Pasadena, dipped his wings, and said over the public address system in the airplane, 'I'm making a prediction. You'll be back here in January, men!'

All the players looked outside at that mammoth bowl of a stadium sitting in the foothills of the California mountains, and they began to think. They began to think roses. I loved that pilot.

# Life at the top

We played our hearts out in 1979. We played for the national title and I was swept away with the excitement of being head football coach at OSU. The effort of those kids was outstanding. The 1979 season started with a big win over Syracuse, then a tough win at Minnesota.

*Raging Buckeye: Exclamation point on the game's grammar*

We beat Washington State at home. The victory

at UCLA was magnificent. Trailing again, we ran

the two-minute drill almost surgically, and won 17-13.

We were a machine.

―――――――――

After getting by Northwestern 16-7, the road seemed to get easier. Near blowouts over Indiana, Wisconsin, Michigan State, Illinois, and Iowa just greased us up for the real game—Michigan. That year, the game was played at Michigan. Before the game, Bo and I talked at midfield. He described how poor their kicking game had been that season, and he had spoken the truth. Michigan's punting was awful, which really helped us in field position situations. For three years, Ohio State had failed to score against Michigan, so my goal was to break that jinx. And we did.

Art Schlichter threw to the split end in the end zone. The ball was tipped, but we caught it somehow. We knocked out starting quarterback B. J. Dickey in the first quarter when Michigan tried to run the option. Then they used a second-string passing quarterback, John Wrangler. He threw one touchdown pass to Anthony Carter and set up another with a long pass.

Michigan had the lead 15-12 in the fourth quarter, and we blocked a punt to win. Jim Laughlin blocked it and Todd Bell ran it in for the winning touchdown. What a crazy game. I remember the hit freshman linebacker Marcus Marek made on Butch Woolfolk, knocking him backwards—a textbook hit that should be in every linebacker's manual. Art Schlichter had a great game, and so did receiver Doug Donley. Our offensive line played well and our defense was exceptional, with the exception of the lone passes to Anthony Carter. We had scored a touchdown, kicked some field goals, and missed some extra points. Tailbacks Jimmy Gayle and Calvin Murray both ran well, but were knocked out of the game.

Tim Spencer, our fourth team tailback, and a true freshman, had to carry the ball as we ran out the clock. He ran for 26 yards and made two first downs. It was a damn impressive victory that put us smackdab right in the middle of the Rose Bowl.

The 1979 game signaled a new shift in the rivalry. It was at Michigan. It was against Bo. That victory broke the jinx of not scoring in three years, capped off an undefeated season, earned us a Big Ten title, and the trip to Pasadena. We had a national championship on the line.

The locker room was jubilant after the game. A couple of the players came up to me and said, 'The pilot was right, Coach.'

They were referring to the airline pilot who dipped his wing over the Rose Bowl after the win at UCLA and announced over the intercom, 'You'll be back here January 1.'

**ALL THAT FOLLOWED THE 1979 MICHIGAN** victory was a story in itself. Roses carpeted the locker room and team buses as we left the stadium bound for the airport and a return flight to Columbus. Scores of scarlet and gray clad fans jammed the locker room exit and the noise was deafening. But it didn't matter to me. We beat Michigan and we were headed to the Rose Bowl. The Buckeye fans deserved to celebrate.

As our chartered plane prepared to land, I could see about twenty Columbus police cruisers out on the runway, lights on, waiting for our arrival. After we taxied to a stop, I left the plane, my arms full of roses and thought to myself, this is pretty doggone nice. Happy fans and police escorts. If this is the way it's going to be—what a career.

One of the escort officers welcomed me by saying, 'We've got a problem, Coach. There are a couple of cars on fire on High Street. Thousands of students and fans are in the street celebrating. It's a mini-riot of sorts and we're going to take you a back way to campus.'

Only then did I finally start to understand why there were so many police cars at the airport. They were worried about our safety. There were several hundred fans on hand at the airport but I couldn't begin to comprehend how bad it must have been around campus. I rode in one of the police cruisers as they escorted us to the practice facility. We stayed a safe distance from High Street. The television film I saw of it was disturbing. To think that our fans and students would start destroying people's property, all in the name of celebrating the Buckeyes' season, was appalling to me.

BEFORE 1979 OFFICIALLY ENDED, I had one last post-Michigan trauma. We were deep into preparations for our Rose Bowl battle with USC when I woke up one night with a terrible wrenching pain throughout my chest.

I woke up Jean and told her something was wrong. She called the team physician, Dr. Bob Murphy. Dr. Bob said he'd send an ambulance, but I didn't want an ambulance. Jean made the eight-minute drive to Riverside Hospital. They put me in a wheelchair when I arrived and quietly proceeded to check me in when I heard one of the women on duty at the ER registration table yell, 'Hey, who is that? Who is that?! Who is that going through there?!'

We didn't stop for anyone, but it was only a few minutes before word spread throughout the emergency room that the Ohio State coach was being treated. And the news flash didn't stop in the ER. After the hospital knew, the whole city of Columbus knew as well.

Doctors at the hospital told me I needed a heart catheter or I couldn't go to the Rose Bowl. He shocked me a little when he told me that one per cent of the people who have this procedure die.

'What the hell do I want this procedure for if one per cent of the people die?' I asked.

All of sudden I felt great. But they insisted and, thankfully, were unable to find anything wrong.

At the next practice, some players came up to me with a diagnosis.

'We know what happened,' they said. 'We saw you eat that chili at the training table. We get indigestion all the time when we eat that stuff.'

I couldn't believe it. I stood there speechless. They were right. I *did* eat chili before bed that night. I was a little embarrassed about all the fuss that chili stirred up. To this day, I have to be cautious of heartburn. Chili almost cost me a trip to the Rose Bowl.

The biggest regret I ever had was not winning the Rose Bowl. It's one of the biggest disappointments in my life. We played our hearts out for that national title in 1979. We were the last Ohio State team to go 11 and 0.

When you look at the personnel we faced in 1979, you start to realize how well our kids played. Charles White, Anthony Munoz, Ronnie Lott. Lott hit Doug Donley so hard on one play it spun his helmet around. I was so disappointed we didn't win that game.

We blew the game on an option play early in the game. On fourth and one, we chose to run, and we lost a yard. If we had pitched the ball, it would have been great, but Art kept the ball and got tackled. If we had kicked the ball, we would have won the game. As it was, we were ahead 16-10 with about five minutes remaining in the game when they drove the length of the football field and won the game 17-16.

We finished 11 and 1. We were the Big Ten champions and the Rose Bowl representatives. I had dealt with the pressure of stepping in for the great Woody Hayes. I thought we would have a successful season, but I didn't know what it would entail. The results of 1979 were tremendous. We went into the Rose Bowl as the number one team in the nation. Everybody said I won with Woody's players, and you know what? They're right. I wasn't left with a bare cupboard, I'll be the first to tell you.

When I got to Ohio State, we had speed, talent, and a good quarterback. The transition was good. And Woody helped with the transition by being very supportive. He never wanted to be a distraction, so he stayed away from the games and from practice. I went to see him every

*⊃Sideline intensity: The coach in a restrained moment*

two weeks at the Military Science Building where he kept his office and kept telling him that whenever he felt comfortable we would love to see him attend a practice and come to a game.

His longtime friend, *Dispatch* sportswriter Paul Hornung finally convinced him to come back to the stadium and we made sure he came in and out with a minimum of attention. I never at all regretted being the coach who succeeded Coach Hayes. I got to be honest with you, at that time I felt I was the guy who could follow Coach Hayes and be successful. If I didn't feel that way I wouldn't have done it. I wasn't going to be the guy who said, 'I want to be the guy who followed the guy who followed Woody.' A person with that attitude is a loser.

¶IN 1980, AFTER THE CLOSE ROSE BOWL LOSS, we were predicted to be number one. Everyone was eager for the season to start. We opened with four straight wins at home before UCLA came in and upset us 17-0. We had a tight end playing tackle in that game because we were hurting along the offensive line. UCLA's big defensive tackle just chewed up our guy and spit him out all day long. Schlichter was nailed in the middle of the back all day long, virtually eliminating our passing attack. Art was hurt and backup quarterback Bob Atha finished the game.

UCLA was really fired up. Their defensive back even slugged one of our assistant coaches, and was thrown out of the game. We were shocked because we thought we would totally dominate the Bruins. They were angry about the year before when we beat them in California and were eager for revenge. Terry Donahue was a young, up-and-coming head coach and he really had them prepared.

We came back, won six games in a row, and headed into the season finale—at home with Michigan. Outstanding Wolverine tailback Butch Woolfolk had a tremendous day, but Michigan still only scored nine points. Unfortunately, that was all they needed.

We moved the ball all day but not effectively. There were fourteen first downs. Michigan held onto the ball and demonstrated great defense. We were the better team but played poorly. It seemed like we were so caught up in the hype of that number one ranking that we didn't think about the game.

We're driving down, with the score 9-3. Second down and six or seven. We run the tailback trap play and the guard comes around to take on the Michigan linebacker. Our guard makes the wrong decision, goes outside, and the linebacker comes inside—the hole was big enough to build a house in—and stuffs Calvin Murray at the line of scrimmage.

The coaches were yelling from the press box, 'Run it again. Run it again, it'll work, it'll work!'

Now here we are, late in the game, trailing 9-3, and it's third and 7. Do you run it? I said, Wait a minute. We have Art Schlichter and all these receivers, why don't we throw the ball? If you throw the ball twice and miss, hey, at least you're giving great effort.

'Coach, the trap will work, it'll work!' they insisted. I made a dumb decision: I called for the trap again. It was a stupid play that I never should have let happen.

I said, 'Up the middle on third down, when we're movin' in and the score is 9 to 3? No way! I don't think we should run it again!'

Glen Mason, upstairs in the pressbox, said it looked like a good play with the middle wide open, so I agreed for us to run it again. This time, Michigan's defense slanted right down, and they stopped us cold. I don't think we ever took into consideration that they would change their defense. We should have run an option pass or run, and I shouldn't have run a trap play up the middle.

We go from having great field position and third and 7, to fourth and 8. Fourth and 8, in my mind, isn't a conversion down. So we go for a field goal, hoping to get three points, hold Michigan, then get the ball back. So we kicked—and missed. Game's over.

Only scoring three points to Michigan and losing at home was heartbreaking. The kids were demoralized. Art Schlichter was more depressed than anyone. Whatever play was called, it should have been something to feature the quarterback. But I didn't do that.

As I walked back into the locker room, one of our diehard, rabid fans was yelling every obscenity possible at me. He was right along the tunnel in my face. He was jumping up and down and screaming like a wild man. A Columbus policeman, Bob Dent, assigned to escort me, turned and said, 'You know, Earle, I think if he had a gun, he'd shoot you.' What that fan didn't realize was that I was just as upset as he was. That was one defeat that should have never happened.

Then we headed into the Fiesta Bowl to play Penn State. The Fiesta Bowl has always been my favorite bowl game. They did special things for the team and treated everyone first class. I think some other bowl games, particularly the Rose Bowl, has been more for administrators. The Fiesta gained popularity after we went there, and, as the word spread, lots of people wanted to go there.

Our only difficulty was that we lost 31-19. We were ahead 19-7 and didn't score in the second half. Penn State pulled a trick play, faking a field goal and scoring a touchdown to put them back in the ball game.

Two losses ended the season, and we had been picked to win it all. 'Nine and three Earle' would become my trademark. As Ohio State's head coach, my record was 9 and 3, every year from 1980 through 1985.

¶IN 1981, ART SCHLICHTER and Glen Cobb were our senior captains and I thought we were in for an outstanding season. We opened with road wins over Duke, Michigan State, and Stanford. Then, Bobby Bowden and Florida State came to Ohio Stadium and beat us 36-27. Art set the individual OSU game record for passing—458 yards.

Then, the following week, we lost at Wisconsin 24-21. About a month later, we lost at Minnesota 35-31. Our safety let the ball go right through his hands on a near interception, and Minnesota took it in for the winning touchdown. Two Big Ten losses by a combined seven points.

The highlight of the season, of course, was the Michigan game. The lead changed hands four times. It was a seesaw. They went ahead 3-0, then we went ahead 7-3. We trailed again in the fourth quarter but finally pulled ahead after two 80-yard drives resulted in touchdowns, and we won 14-9.

The last drive featured Art Schlichter completing a long pass on third down to Tim Spencer. Tim then executed a 19-yard pitch sweep around the end, and then the patented Schlichter touchdown into a snowbank in Michigan's end zone to win it, 14-9.

Schlichter played like a demon. He took the ball on the six-yard line, cut in, cut out, went behind a great block by fullback Vaughn Broadnax on Michigan's defensive end, eluded four tacklers, and went into the corner of the end zone for the score. What a way to salvage a season.

Timmy Spencer had a hell of an exhibition running the football that day. He caught a 50-yard pass on the last play, a broken play. We intercepted four passes, and did one helluva job on Anthony Carter. We also kept the ball away from him on kicks —until the last one, a line drive kick right to him. Old number one started racing full speed right at us, up the middle of the field.

Finally, we knocked him out of bounds between the 35 and 40 yard lines, but, boy, was I sweating. For a minute, I thought I was going to have to tackle him. With a game-breaker on the field like Anthony Carter lots of things can go wrong fast. He won a lot of games for the Wolverines on the last play of the game. That day, they settled for three field goals.

Every Friday before the Michigan game, the boosters group held a Michigan pregame luncheon. It was obvious no one thought we would win. *Football News* had written earlier in the week that Bo could name his score against Ohio State because we were in such a state of disarray after losing at Minnesota two weeks prior.

I knew one thing: *Football News* hadn't been coming to our practices. When I went into that booster group, all the faces were long and hanging to the tabletops. They sensed disaster. They had already lost the game. No smiles, no nothing. I knew damn well they didn't want to hear from Earle Bruce. So I walked up to the podium and gave them the standard greeting. Then I said, 'I know you people out there have already lost this football game. But I want to tell you something. You're going to be shocked how well we play up there tomorrow.'

That was my shortest speech ever to Buckeye Boosters. We played better than I ever could have predicted. It was a hell of a win for Ohio State. Those kids played like they were possessed. We had two 80-yard drives. As always, Marcus Marek played tremendously. Joe Lukens was outstanding. Art had a good game, and so did Tim Spencer and receiver Gary Williams. The key to the Michigan game is to have your great players play great. And they did.

We went to the Liberty Bowl that year and beat Navy 31-28. Memphis was like one big Navy pep rally all week. All the Naval people were there, and it was far from a neutral gathering. Our kids didn't even want to go to Memphis. They couldn't understand how we missed the top prize.

We beat Michigan, and yet they went to the Bluebonnet Bowl. Iowa goes to the Rose Bowl, and we go to the Liberty Bowl. We didn't play Iowa that year because of one of those Big Ten scheduling quirks. We had to play four non-conference games, but we couldn't play Iowa because Iowa had a schedule conflict with Iowa State. If we could have played Iowa, *we* would have gone to the Rose Bowl.

¶QUARTERBACK PROBLEMS marked the start of the 1982 season after the departure of Art Schlichter. Mike Tomczak was the starter, and we opened the season with wins at home against Baylor and on the road at Michigan State. Then John Elway and Stanford came into Columbus for the third game of the season and beat us 23-20.

I told defensive coordinator Bob Tucker the way to stop Elway was not to stand back and play iffy-iffy with him in a prevent defense. The way to play Elway was to go get him. Put everyone in the blitz and get his ass, otherwise, he'll pick you apart.

We were ahead 20-16, and got the ball with about a minute to go, second or third and long. All we have to do is get one more first down. But they're playing good defense, and we've been having problems running the ball.

⊃*Life in the trenches: A gesture from on high*

We take a time out and I tell Tomczak we're going to run Play Pass 28. But, he is NOT to throw the ball. He's to keep it and run. Make the fake, roll out, and keep the ball. Our goal was to break, contain, and run. Then go down with the ball after the first down. We talk about the play, the time-out is coming to a conclusion, and Tomczak runs back out onto the field.

'Mike!' I yelled one more time. I'm yelling as loud as I can. 'Don't throw the football. You understand that? Don't throw the football!'

Once the play starts, Mike rolls out. It looks like clear sailing for a first down. He's starting to run, and all of the sudden he sees Gary Williams coming free on the post pattern. So, along with 90,000 others, I watch as Tomczak stops, takes a step or two back, and fires it—with a little loft. Stanford's safety man comes over and makes the interception in the end zone.

Elway was virtually unchallenged on the final drive and completed a big 50-yarder to seal the win. It started a string of three straight home losses. Florida State beat us 34-17, and Wisconsin beat us 6-0. I benched Tomczak in that game. My thinking was that if we lost three with him as a sophomore starting quarterback, his confidence would be so shaken his career might have been over. He would have been heartbroken. So I started a transfer from Massillon, Brent Offenbacher.

Our kids told me Brent was not ready to play, and, frankly, we didn't have a good effort. It was a rainy day, and even though we had a chance to win, Wisconsin was successful in keeping the ball away from us, and we could never get going.

THE FOLLOWING THURSDAY, before the Illinois game, President Jennings came to practice to speak to the team. We practiced in the stadium and he said to the kids, 'It doesn't matter if you win this game or not. Don't feel you're under any pressure. Nothing is going to happen whether you win this football game or not.'

I was shell shocked. What the hell kind of speech is this to a team of football players? He's taking this real soft approach, and after he was done

I walked over to the players and said, 'Whoa. I want you to know something right now, fellas. It's *damn* important that we win this football game. Beating Illinois is damn important to everyone of you. Do you want to be a member of the worst football team in the history of Ohio State? That's where you're headed. We've got to go over there and win that football game. You can't think about anything else.'

I'm sure my comments might have upset the President, but I really didn't give a damn. That game was important and we won it when Mike Tomczak threw a game-winning touchdown to Thad Jemison. The score was 26-21 and I've always said that's the game Mike Tomczak became a quarterback.

We won the rest of the schedule, and finished up with Michigan in Columbus. We dominated the game, but we had to rally and score 10 points in the fourth quarter to win it, 24-14. Marcus Marek had 21 tackles. We caused a crucial fumble late in the game when Michigan ran the ISO option to Anthony Carter, we hit Carter and got the ball. Marek intercepted a pass. He intercepted a pass in every Michigan game he played.

Most of the Michigan games are won or lost in the fourth quarter, and this was no exception. Michigan's record was 8 and 1, and OSU was 7 and 1. Since we couldn't schedule Iowa again, Michigan went to the Rose Bowl. What moronic scheduling! We were kept out of the Rose Bowl for two straight years, through no fault of our own.

I've often wondered if I was out of my mind for not speaking up publicly about this asinine foul-up. What a crock. We won three of four games against Michigan, and we only went to the Rose Bowl once.

Still, we ended up as strong as any team in the country that year. The grand finale was beating BYU in the Holiday Bowl in San Diego, 47-17. Tim Spencer was a workhorse out of the backfield, and Tomczak did a great job throwing the ball. We were a physical, dominating team.

¶WE OPENED THE 1983 SEASON WITH A 31-6 WIN over the Oregon Ducks, setting the stage for a huge first test of the season, on the road, against Barry Switzer's Oklahoma Sooners. Everyone remembered when Oklahoma came into Columbus in 1977 and won in the rain 29-28 on that last-minute field goal. It was a game that many considered one of the best games ever played at Ohio Stadium.

We went to Oklahoma, played very well, and won 24-14. Our defense rallied behind Pepper Johnson. Roland Tatum had a helluva game with a fumble recovery while leading the team in tackles. Tailback Keith Byars played an exceptional game, as did Tomczak, who threw for 234 yards.

At one point we had them 24-7. We knocked their great running back, Marcus Dupree, out of the game. Dupree ran for 225 yards the year before in the Fiesta Bowl. I knew Keith Byars could make Marcus Dupree look average, and that's exactly what happened.

John Frank caught two touchdown passes. When you see it on tape, the two plays look almost identical. He caught seven passes for 108 yards. He was questionable for that game because it was a Jewish holiday, but his Dad worked it out so he could play.

John wasn't very big as a tight end goes, but he could run and he could block. He caught between 45 and 50 passes each year for two years at Ohio State, holding OSU's record for tight ends. He was the leading receiver, catching the 'Y-shallow.' And if he hit you and got his feet moving, he'd take you off the planet.

John was a great recruiting story out of Mt. Lebanon, Pennsylvania. I recruited that area along with assistant coach Steve Szabo. Steve was tenacious in pursuing John. I finally told Steve, 'Get off him, he's going to Pitt.'

'I'm not getting off him,' Steve said.

'You're wasting your time,' I said.

Damn if we didn't turn him around and get him to Ohio State. He wanted to be an orthopedic surgeon. His interest in A's and B's exceeded his interest in X's and O's.

The last week of the season when we were playing Michigan, he finally said to me, 'Coach, I want to be an All-Pro tight end.'

I was shocked. 'What?' I said. 'All you've ever talked about was being a doctor!'

'Yeah,' he said, 'but I want to be an All-Pro tight end for a few years, first.'

'I've been telling all the scouts and everybody that you're not going to play pro ball because you want to become a doctor!' I said.

So he proceeds to get drafted, wears two Super Bowl rings, and is now an ear-nose-throat doctor in Chicago. With his pro career at its peak, John gave it up to realize his other ambition. He was afraid a hand injury in pro ball might block his life's goal. I truly admired and related to John Frank. I was brought up that you went to college for an education, then football, and I wanted players to attend Ohio State University for a degree before all else.

THE OKLAHOMA GAME was the ultimate team victory because everyone played so hard, away from home, and it was 114 degrees on the field. As a result of the game, Mike Tomczak spent several days in the hospital with heat exhaustion. He went into the Iowa game the next week and couldn't throw. He threw the ball into the ground on the passing attack and had three interceptions. Iowa wound up winning, 20 to 14.

Chuck Long was at quarterback and they performed well. Illinois beat us in their stadium, 17-13. Tomczak suffered a concussion, said he could continue to play, but he was out of it. I finally took him out of the game. He didn't know what was going on. Even so, we led 13-10 with 1:47 left. Illinois then marched 83 yards in just five plays and beat Ohio State for the first time since 1967. Illinois had a great team that year and won all nine of their Big Ten games.

That was the year former Indiana coach Sam Wyche gave me the finger after we won at Indiana, 56-17. What a classy gesture, huh? Jim Karsotas was our third-team quarterback, and he completed a 63-yard touchdown pass for our final touchdown. Wyche wouldn't let his players shake our players' hands after the game, and he gave me the finger across the field. I couldn't believe my eyes. I chuckled, recognizing in the heat of battle people sometimes do some bizarre things. I wanted to ask Woody if he ever thought Rommel gave Montgomery the finger across the desert.

**THE LAST GAME WAS IN ANN ARBOR,** the usual OSU-Michigan game, down to the wire. At one point, we held a 14-10 lead, and used a trick play where Tomczak takes the ball and puts it down on the ground behind the center. Left guard Jim Lachey was to pick it up and go. I used to watch Nebraska execute that play to perfection. So we practiced it all season because Jim Lachey had a lot of speed. He would be the kind of guy that could walk into the end zone with that kind of play. But we never practiced it full-go, like we should have.

When I made the call of the infamous Lachey Left, Michigan's defense jammed the center, and the ball was booted a little and became a 'free' ball. The play was one of those that shone when it worked and caused chaos when it didn't. It was a classic example of thinking about the quick touchdown instead of concentrating on earning the touchdown through good, consistent drives. We had failed to control the line of scrimmage, and Michigan got too much penetration. We were in the game, we were moving the ball, and we should have stuck with our regular offense.

We had three fumbles in that game and lost two of them. That was the difference. Michigan had one fumble and NO turnovers. 'Lachey Left' made me realize that in that game, you need to play football. Using tricks is a dangerous idea. You block, tackle, run to the ball, and play good defense. Nothing out of the ordinary.

I don't want to take anything away from Michigan. They played exceptionally well, and that was only one bad play. When you look at the stats of that Michigan game, we had 298 yards passing and 150 yards rushing. That's a lot of yards to end up with only 21 points. Michigan won by a field goal—24-21—because we made too many turnovers. We gained good yardage but lost the ball too many times. I vowed never

*⊃Hat in hand: An uncharacteristic pose for the coach*

to use one of those trick plays ever again in a Michigan game.

We finished—again—with three losses. Then we beat Pittsburgh 28-23 in the Fiesta Bowl. Pittsburgh was ahead with less than a minute to go, and President Jennings decided this would be a good time to fire Hugh Hindman as athletic director so he could bring in his own guy. And I was supposed to be fired, too. But Mike Tomczak threw a touchdown pass to Thad Jemison on the last play of the game, and that toss stopped my firing.

The talk around Columbus was that President Jennings and his wife thought Hindman had fired *me*. Jennings' wife—now ex-wife—actually came up to my wife, Jean, and said, 'I'm sorry to hear what happened.'

My wife, of course, didn't know what Mrs. Jennings was talking about. I was still safe, the talk around Columbus was that President Jennings wanted to dump the athletic director, the football and basketball coaches, and bring in his own people. Ultimately, of course, that's exactly what happened.

¶**MIKE TOMCZAK BROKE HIS LEG** in the 1984 spring game, and I inserted Jim Karsotas. Within five minutes I got a message from Woody Hayes, who was sitting in the stands.

'You get Karsotas out of there. Don't you play Karsotas. If you play Karsotas, you might not have a quarterback next year if something happens to him. You get him out of the game.'

I thought, my God, he's right. Karsotas is the only experienced QB now. But Tomczak worked his ass off to get back. He worked, ran, sharpened his lateral movement across the field, and endured the two-a-days.

As we neared the first game, it was obvious he was spent. Our team doctor, Dr. Bob Murphy, told me he needed more time to heal. So I called him into my office and said maybe the best thing was to red-shirt that season.

'I want to graduate with the seniors,' he told me. 'That's my group. And I'm going to play football.'

Dr. Bob said he didn't know if he'd be able to or not, so we X-rayed him right away and there was a tiny piece of separation in the foot. We couldn't play him in the first game. But in two weeks time, when we X-rayed him again, that gap had closed. Dr. Bob said as long as he wore a little protection device he could play. He played like man who appreciated a second chance.

The season also marked the debut of linebacker Chris Spielman, the freshman from Massillon. In high school, he played tailback, linebacker, special teams, and even sold popcorn in the stands.

**I'VE NEVER SEEN ANYONE PLAY** high school football like Chris Spielman. They even launched a successful campaign in Massillon to have him put on the cover of the Wheaties Box. But at OSU, he was only a freshman, and he was on the sidelines.

He was hotly recruited by the best schools in the land, and I thought Michigan or Miami of Florida would lure him from Ohio. Glen Mason, my offensive coordinator and assistant head coach, and I spent a lot of time recruiting Spielman. The night before national signing date, I went to Massillon watch him play basketball. He hadn't made a final decision, and he promised to call me before midnight with his choice. I drove back to Columbus at 11:30 p.m. and went to bed just after midnight. I felt sick because I'd never heard a word from him.

I was in a deep sleep when Chris called at 1:30 a.m.

'Hi, Coach,' he says. 'I've made my decision.'

'Good,' I said.

There was a pause that seemed to last the rest of the night. I thought to myself, oh, my God, he's struggling to tell me he's going to Michigan.

Finally, he said—and softly—'I'm gonna be a Buckeye!'

My heart started pounding. I whooped and yelled, 'That's GREAT! Congratulations! We're glad to have you. You'll have a great career here. You'll be an All-American!'

Then I said, 'You son-of-a-gun. You just made my heart skip a beat.

I know you played this up to get me rattled. When you get down here, I'm gonna kick your ass.'

### HE LAUGHED; THE REST IS HISTORY.

I knew I could say that to him. We had a great relationship from the early days. His physical size wasn't that imposing, but his presence was intimidating for any opponent. His passion for the game was legendary. He had twisted his ankle during practice for the Ohio High School All-Star game, and his pre-season performance was mediocre. He was second team and we weren't planning on playing him against Oregon State.

We're trailing Oregon State 14-6 near the end of the first half, and Oregon State was marching down the field when I hear all this noise behind me on the bench.

'I've got to play! I've got to play! I've got to get in the game!'

I look back and there's Spielman with his head down, stomping. He's like a raging bull, stalking up and down. He's so loud, I'm hearing him through my headsets. I thought to myself, holy shit, I've never seen anyone act like this on the sideline.

I tapped defensive coordinator Bob Tucker on the shoulder and said, 'Bob, when are you going to play Chris?'

Tucker took off his headsets and said, 'What did you say?'

'When are you going to play Chris Spielman?' I said again. He says, 'Coach, he's a freshman. He's got a bad ankle. I don't know whether he's ready or not.'

'*Listen* to him,' I said to Bob. 'He's *ready*. I'm afraid to leave him over here on the bench. If we don't put him in the game, he might hurt one of *us*.'

We trail Oregon State 14-6 at halftime, and I gave Bob Tucker an ultimatum. 'Bob, I'm ordering you to play Chris Spielman in the second half. Start him! If you don't want to do it, you can leave.'

'OK, Coach,' he said. 'He'll play.'

We had to bench Pepper Johnson. That's how 'organized' we were. We had 'em both playing the same position. How crazy was that? So

Spielman comes in, Pepper Johnson comes out, and I'm watching the first ten plays of the second half—three series.

He makes the first ten tackles. I never saw anybody like that in my life. Running through guys, going over guys, knocking them back. You could hear the entire stadium react to his play. I thought to myself, 'Holy Hell!' He turned the entire game around, and we won the dogfight.

Chris taught me what intensity looked like in football. He loved the physical aspects of the game. He took coaching. He could communicate as well as listen. You could count on him to go to class. Chris wasn't out in the High Street bars on the weekends. He had fun, but football was his consuming passion. He always has and always will set a standard for pure love of the game. If he decides to pursue a career in coaching, he will be a great one.

Because of his love of the game, I predict he will always be connected with football in some way. The cliches about 'heart' in sports are overused. But when he reached the pros—filled with seventh- and eighth-round draft picks who made it because of heart—he defined again the intangible heart of the consummate athlete.

**THE NEXT WEEK WE DID EVERYTHING RIGHT** against Washington State, winning 44-0. Next, we beat Iowa 45-26, and then Minnesota 35-22. Then we go to Purdue. They beat us 28-23. There were a couple of interesting stories out of that game. Purdue scored on the first possession, in part because three of our defensive starters were out due to a 'violation of team rules.' Which was really some drug activity.

That was also the day of the 'lost down.' We're moving the ball at the end of the ball game and throw a nice completion to Cris Carter for about 25 yards. He gets hit and knocked out of bounds, under our bench. When he comes out, the official throws a flag on him and said he retaliated for being knocked under the bench.

It was a 15-yard penalty from where he caught the ball. I said, 'What? He *retaliated*? If I look at the film and he 'retaliated', he will pay for it like you're not gonna believe!' We got that film, and where this guy saw anybody retaliate I don't really know. In fact, the official was 'rested' the following week and not given an assignment for the next game because of that call. He should have been fired for calling something that no one could see.

Now, it's fourth down. We're moving the football. Time is becoming critical. Their down marker on the side has third down, while the scoreboard has fourth down. But the scoreboard is changed late, and the man on the sideline doesn't see it. Tomczak tries to call a time-out, but we don't have any more time-outs. Tomczak looks at the sideline marker, and runs a play that's not going anywhere. He kills the ball on fourth down—throwing the ball up in the stands. That's the game.

We came back against Illinois and win, 45-38. And Illinois was up 24-0 in the first quarter. We did try a couple of trick plays in that ball game to get back in it. We tried an on-side kick and got it back. We tried an end-around or flanker around, throwing it to Cris Carter, and he dives and catches it on the two. Keith Byars ran out of his shoe on a long touchdown run and had 274 yards.

Then we beat Michigan State up there, but we lost at Wisconsin, 16-14. We beat Indiana and Northwestern, then turned to face Michigan. What I recall most about that game was Rhodes Scholar Mike Lanese's fourth-quarter catch when we were leading 7-6, and he jumped over the stadium to haul in a third-down dig route pass and keep our drive alive. Pepper Johnson had a huge fumble recovery, which led to the final touchdown, and we won, 21-6. And I earned my second trip to the Rose Bowl as head coach.

**MIKE LANESE CAME TO OHIO STATE** as a running back from outside of Cleveland. His dad played with Bo Schembechler at Miami of Ohio, so we had to beat out Michigan for his services. Mike was one of only two Rhodes Scholars in the history of Ohio State. He was the best-read athlete I've ever known. And everything he read, he retained. His major concern was academics. Did we have an emphasis on academics? How much time did we take for football? He was always able to manage his time, performing in an extraordinary fashion both in the classroom and on the field.

His hands were so good, we decided to make him a wide receiver. The problem was that he didn't like the change. He fought us on it until he started mastering the moves, and making the cuts. He was the right size, and we knew he would be a great wide receiver.

He was extremely serious. You could not kid Mike Lanese. You could be ribbing him, and he'd never know it. I was walking into my office one day before practice and here he comes. I could see by the worried look on his face that he was troubled deeply about something.

He charges up to me and says, 'I know you guys. I know what you're up to!'

I asked him what in the hell he was talking about.

'I hear everything,' he said. 'I know you're going to move me to defensive back!'

'Mike,' I said, 'what in God's name are you talking about?'

He was emphatic.

'I *heard* it. They're trying to recruit me right now. Someone's over there talking to me about playing defensive back. Are you trying to move me?'

I looked him right in the eye and told him we had no plans to move him from wide receiver.

'You can count on that, OK?' I said. 'I'm telling you right now. Get it out of your head. There's some guys putting you on, Michael. Those guys want to pull your chain a little bit. You fell for it.'

He looked sheepishly at me, and his voice trailed off.

There was a concentrated effort by the University for him to become a Rhodes Scholar. The school launched a superlative lobbying effort, and Michael was brilliant in all his interview situations. To me, however, Mike's most brilliant moment was his superhuman leap that allowed us to win the Michigan game.

'Everyone is going to remember you as a Rhodes Scholar but me,'

I told him. 'I'm always going to remember you for the third-and-6 play against Michigan.'

In the Rose Bowl against USC, we took the opening drive down the field, and after an offside call, settled for a field goal. We played bad football the first half of that game. We were down 17-9, only to come back in the second half and make it a 20-17 ball game, which is how the game ended.

We weren't mentally ready to play football and it showed. Not to take anything away from USC, but we should have beaten them. However, we didn't play football, and they did. It's hard for me to believe a team is not ready to play in the Rose Bowl, but we made some simple mistakes that shouldn't have been made.

Our kids faced a lot of distractions out there. That's always a coach's fear at the Rose Bowl. Instead of worrying about the game plan, the kids think about trips to Knott's Berry Farm or how much prime rib they can eat at the prime rib competition. It manifests itself in the game when someone jumps offside, or the quarterback turns and runs the wrong way on a play—mistakes you should never make in the Rose Bowl. We weren't focused.

KEITH BYARS HAD A GREAT JUNIOR YEAR IN '84, running for about 1,700 yards. He should have been a Heisman recipient. He could run. He could pass. He was one great athlete. He was a great baseball and basketball player, and he even ran track. Everyone will remember Keith kicking his shoe off in the Illinois game and still running for a touchdown—diving over from the four-yard line into the end zone. He possessed great innate talent for football, and he should have won the Heisman trophy as a junior. I was told by a television network insider that many network people were from Boston College and the television highlights of Doug Flutie's infamous 'Hail Mary' pass would get him in. So Keith was nosed out by a Hail Mary.

When he went to the television taping of the Bob Hope show with the preseason All-American team, agents were all over him, trying to get him to set an example of juniors leaving school for the NFL draft. Fortunately, that didn't happen, and as a senior, Keith would have been a top contender for the Heisman, but he broke the fifth metatarsal bone in his foot. In order to salvage his season, we tried to bring him along slowly, keeping him out for seven or eight weeks. He re-injured the foot at Minnesota, which ended his college career.

¶WE OPENED 1985 WITH WINS OVER PITTSBURGH, Colorado, and Washington State. Pittsburgh had a great defensive team and played us tougher than hell in our stadium. We kicked a field goal and Cris Carter caught a touchdown pass for a 10-7 win.

During Colorado week, my dad, Earl, passed away and I flew home for a few days and rejoined the team on Friday. He suffered from Alzheimer's and was in a nursing home where he contracted pneumonia. After being hospitalized and placed on life support, my mother made the decision to pull the plug. I had spent a week with him in July when he was in pretty bad shape in the nursing home. I was named for my Dad and loved him dearly. My Mom put the 'e' on the end of my first name, but Dad's name was spelled the common E-A-R-L. It was near impossible to keep your mind on football when you have a loss in real life.

The coaches and the kids were great. Everybody knew about my situation and pulled together, allowing me the time to go to my dad. I was pretty subdued. When I returned, it was hard to get back into the game. Football was such a way of life that sometimes I had to remind myself it was—at its core—a game.

I called the offensive plays, but I was in a fog. We just kept running the tailback and did the fullback trap and the things necessary to get through the game. For once I didn't feel the game was the most important thing in the world. I was physically on the job, but that was about it.

John Woolridge had a hell of a day in Colorado and went through holes like you couldn't believe, picking up five and six yards when there wasn't even a hole. Bill McCartney ran the wishbone at Colorado, but we dominated them. Washington State ran the ball well, but we had too much offense and won, 48-32. The next week we went to Illinois and played in some of the windiest conditions I can ever remember. All the scoring was done with the wind favoring you.

They jumped out to a 14-0 lead, and we tied it. We had a 28-14 lead and they tied it. They had the ball last, with the wind, and from about the 30-yard line, kicked a field goal to win, 31-28. I was sick. We played hard and long and in wicked wind conditions. It was the worst game condition I've ever played or coached in. The outcome was decided by the whim of the wind—not skill.

We went on to beat Purdue and Iowa, Minnesota and Northwestern, then we lost to Wisconsin, 12-7. Second year in a row we lost to Wisconsin. Then came Michigan. Late in the fourth quarter in Ann Arbor, we scored and pulled within a field goal, at 17-20. After the scoring drive, we kicked off. On the possession, they are faced with a third and long when quarterback Jim Harbaugh connected on an 80-yard touchdown.

Michigan had speed at the wide out position, we were a little late on the blitz, and we gave Harbaugh time to deliver. It was that close—again. But our performance personified the saying, 'Too little, too late.'

We went to the Citrus Bowl and beat BYU 10-7, the least number of points BYU had ever scored in a game. Our only score came when Larry Kolic, one of our great defensive linemen, intercepted a pass and ran it in 15 or 20 yards for a touchdown. Jim Karsotas didn't have a good day, but we shut them down defensively. We rushed two, dropped everybody else, and snagged five interceptions.

¶WE DECIDED TO START THE 1986 SEASON by playing in the Kickoff Classic. I wasn't in favor of it, but President Jennings wanted to go and so we went. I always thought if you started to play too many games too early in the season, you could take the emphasis off the Michigan game at the end of the season. Which is, of course, something you never want to do at Ohio State. The emphasis should *always* be the Michigan game. Anything that detracts from playing Michigan is not healthy for the football program.

꩜*No chinstrap: Cris Carter models new headware at OSU*

It makes for a long season when you start two weeks ahead of time. There are already enough games and enough pressure for the players. We played Alabama on August 27, 1986, and lost 16-10. We were going into the end zone, ran a trap play, and dropped the football. At the end of the game, Alabama couldn't help but foul Cris Carter when we threw to him. I remember thinking we probably should have thrown more often to him. He was an exceptional receiver, and when he got open he could hurt Alabama. They called pass interference against him two or three times at the end of the game.

The following week we went to Washington and got waxed 40 to 7.

Then we returned home to play Colorado and beat them 13-10 for our first win of the year. Utah came next. We beat them 64-6 but it could have been 104 to 6. It was probably the worst football team I've ever seen. It was a great practice session for us, and anyone who dressed in a uniform played.

We played Illinois and shut 'em down, 14-0. We played Indiana, which had started to become a good football team under Bill Mallory, my colleague and former assistant from Woody's '68 national championship team. We beat them, 24-22. We were behind at halftime, and Cris Carter jumped up on the table in the locker room and says, 'Indiana's never gonna beat us while I'm playin' here! My brother went to school here, and they'll never beat me!'

He went out and made one of the most sensational one-handed catches I had ever seen. We threw him a comeback and he caught the football right before he went out of bounds. That set up the game winning touchdown. In the second half, he played like he was possessed.

No one I've ever coached received ovations from his teammates in practice like Cris Carter did. He made spectacular catches every day that amazed the mere mortals around him. He'd make a catch and all you could do was applaud. You'd say, 'How in the hell did he catch that?'

Coming out of high school, they said he was too slow. What a joke. And he had great hands. Freshman year against Oregon State, we throw a little 'X shallow', coming across the middle about six yards deep. He dropped the ball.

I asked the guy next to me on the sideline, the guy carrying my headphone cord, 'Did he drop that ball? I've NEVER seen Cris Carter drop a ball. Did he drop that ball?!'

'Coach,' he said, 'he dropped that ball!'

'Run that same play again,' I told the coaches. We ran the play again, he caught it, and took off down the field. After the game, I asked him, 'Cris, what happened to you on that first play when you dropped the ball?'

He said, 'Coach, there were 90,000 people in that stadium. Here I am, a freshman coming across the middle. I said to myself, *keep your eye on the ball*. All of sudden, I saw a guy coming at me, and I took my eye off the ball, and I dropped it.'

I don't remember him ever being a freshman again.

**WE WENT THROUGH** the rest of the schedule, beating Purdue, Minnesota, Iowa, Northwestern, and Wisconsin. And then came Michigan week.

The buzz all that week was that quarterback Jim Harbaugh had predicted Michigan would beat us. He shot his mouth off, guaranteeing Bo a victory. Bo didn't seem to mind, and Harbaugh was as good as his word—he played a great game and Michigan won, 26-24.

Our defense didn't play well all day. Jamie Morris gained over 220 yards across our defensive left side. We made great yardage all day, too, which set up an effective passing attack. We really beat ourselves with mistakes, and they controlled the game.

I wanted to pass to Carter instead of kicking that 41-yard field goal. I wanted one more play for Carter to try and use up some yardage before we had to kick. But we didn't have time. Matt Franz kicked a pretty good kick, but it veered just a little wide to the left. Somebody told me after the game they thought I was upset that Franz missed the field goal.

'You know,' I said. 'I never get upset over missing a 41-yard field goal. That's not a chip shot.'

So Michigan was history, and we went to Cotton Bowl to face Texas A & M and Jackie Sherrill. Texas A & M's program under Jackie Sherrill wasn't regarded very highly. It's the only time each coach in the opponent's conference contacted me and said, 'We hope you beat the hell out of Texas A & M.'

The reason for bitterness was that A&M had a quarterback who, most people felt, received a lot of 'incentives' to play at Texas A & M. Meanwhile, A & M was being investigated by the NCAA for recruiting violations. It ultimately cost Sherrill his job and the program was shut down for awhile.

The Cotton Bowl marked the debut of the infamous 'fedora.' *Columbus Dispatch* columnist Mike Harden had written a column about how poorly I dressed and what a poor representation I was standing on the sideline. As a result of that, Athletic Director Rick Bay and I said that maybe I should dress up in a suit coat and tie, like I did when I coached in high school.

Bay said, 'I'll get you a tux and we'll do a limo and the whole bit.' I told him that wasn't exactly me. But I did have a tailor at the old Walker's in Columbus. Maybe I would dress up for Texas A & M. So I got a new suit and a hat at Walker's in Upper Arlington, and smuggled it all to the Cotton Bowl so no one knew about it.

The only two people who knew were my wife and the manager, who put it in the locker. We went out for warm-ups, and I was dressed in coaching gear as always. I paced around and wondered to myself whether I should really do this or not. Then I thought, the hell with it. I walked into the locker room, talked to the team, locked the dressing room door behind me, and put on my outfit.

I came out and walked up and down the aisles and talked individually to the kids and you know what? Not one of the players said a word. Not, 'Coach, what the hell are you doing?' Not, 'Wow, Coach, you look great!' Not one word from any one of them. I thought, 'Here I am dressed up and they don't even *know* I'm dressed up.'

So here we are, ready to go out on the field. I normally lead, but I told them to just go ahead. Truthfully, I was a little dejected. I came out in the middle of the team and started making a decision on the coin toss. I started to yell something about the wind, and assistant coach Tom Lichtenberg said to one of the other assistants, 'Who's that guy down there with the hat on? Why don't they get him off the field?'

The other assistant told him it was me.

'That's Coach Bruce?!'

A couple of my friends watching on television back home told me when the cameras finally focused in on me, my one friend gasped, fell on his knees, and yelled for his wife to come in and see what was going on.

Here's Earle Bruce—all dressed up and with a *hat*. We also debuted our red shoes. A little gimmick from Nike. We were supposed to be able to keep the red shoes, but we had to return them later when we found out we had gone over the limit of gifts to the kids. We won the Cotton Bowl, 28-12. And I decided to dress up for some of the big games from then on.

I wound up with about eighteen hats. I still have most of them. Some I've donated to charity, and they've raised thousands of dollars. The original fedora I gave to a father who was trying to raise some money for his little girl's hospital bills. I also wrote a note explaining the history of the fedora. I even asked my daughter to go to the function and bid up the item so I wouldn't be embarrassed, although it raised the possibility of me ending up with the hat again. But a doctor looked at the item, and said he wouldn't bid on it unless my handwritten note was included. He bought it for just under $5,000.

**THE 1986 SEASON HAD ITS QUOTIENT OF SURPRISES.**
The game with Texas A & M resulted in a job offer at Arizona. With the clarity of hindsight, I've often thought if I had accepted that job, how much easier life would have been. At the time, I had a problem. I really didn't want to leave Ohio State. But I came close to heading west, closer than most people ever knew.

The athletic director from Arizona, Cedric Dempsey, called me the day after the Cotton Bowl. He wanted me to come out and visit. We were still in Texas, and on the return flight I said to OSU Athletic Director Rick Bay, 'Rick, the University of Arizona has contacted me, and they're going to send a plane to Columbus for me to come and visit.'

Bay said, 'I don't want you to go, Earle. I don't want you to go.'

I was fairly insistent and told him, 'I'm going to go talk to them. You know I love Ohio State, but I still want to talk to them.'

I knew I was in trouble with President Jennings. I could tell when we won the game at Texas A & M, and we walked off the field. He wasn't very happy. He clearly acted like I was not the guy he wanted to walk off the field with. The signs were emerging that he was out to remove me, just like Hugh. I owed it to myself and my family to protect myself and see what Arizona had to offer. Later, I found out Rick Bay went to Jennings and told him I had a chance to talk with Arizona and what did he want to do about it. The response, I'm told, was, 'Well, if he goes, he goes.' He wasn't going to do anything to keep me.

So I went to Arizona and enjoyed the red carpet treatment. Cedric offered me a first-class employment package, which would have made me an instant millionaire. Salaries, bonuses, a housing allotment of $60,000 to $80,000 per year for four or five years. All that, plus they were nice people to work with. I was offered the job while in Arizona. From their campus, they flew me to the NCAA coaches convention.

While there, I thought about the opportunity and called Cedric. I accepted the job. When word got out back to Columbus that I was 'thinking' about going to Arizona, my phone began to ring. My assistant coaches and senior-to-be linebacker Chris Spielman all voiced their objections.

Still in San Diego, my assistant coaches came to my hotel room to talk with me, along with Athletic Director Rick Bay. I buckled and called Cedric and I told him I'd reconsidered. I wasn't going to take the job. What a colossal mistake. I had declined an offer-of-a lifetime from Arizona, and I would be fired within the year.

¶IRONICALLY, WHILE MY OWN DRAMA is playing out in 1987, another drama is underway. Cris Carter is working with a sports agent. We lose his eligibility for 1987, and there goes the championship. We lost Nate Harris, who caught seven passes in the Cotton Bowl, then disappeared and ultimately flunked out of school. Tom Tupa was our quarterback, a great passer with no star receivers.

We started out by beating West Virginia and Oregon. We traveled to LSU in a horrific setting, played hard, and settled with a 13-13 tie. We beat Illinois 10-6, but then our recipe for success turned sour. The next week, Indiana upset us at home, 31-10. It rained all day. They controlled the game to the point that we didn't even look like we were playing the same game. I pronounced it a dark day in Ohio State football history, but perhaps it wasn't because whatever we were playing didn't seem to *be* football.

And my good friend Bill Mallory really got mad at me for that declaration. He thought I was taking a cheap shot at his program. That was never my intent. I was bitterly disappointed in our performance that day. I was so depressed and dejected after that game, that is honestly how I felt.

Indiana had a plan. They used their receiver, brought him in motion across zone coverage, and ran him down the field and hooked him 15 or 20 yards behind our linebackers. The quarterback made a little fake and threw to him. It seemed to have worked all day long. Every time they needed a 'possession down', they used that play and we weren't able to adjust. They ate us alive with that pass. Then they held us to only 10 points with good defense. Indiana put us away quickly and kept us down. That day, there was no doubt who was the better football team.

The other game we suffered through was the late-day game with Michigan State at home. MSU came into Columbus and beat us 13-7. On the very first play of the game, we threw a 65-yard touchdown pass to Everett Ross. They came back, held us scoreless, and beat us. Then we traveled to Wisconsin, committed five turnovers, and lost 26-24. We missed a chip shot field goal—from the 15-yard line— at the end of the game, which should have won it for us.

We lost to Iowa, 29-27, for our third straight loss. On the last play of the game, they're on the 35-yard line with fourth down and threw the ball to the 17-yard line. The tight end catches the ball and runs in for a touchdown. Unbelievable. They didn't even throw it into the end zone, and they beat us.

That loss was the decision-maker for Jennings. That's when I was told board of trustee member Debbie Casto came out of the trustees' box at the stadium and pronounced to all the world, 'It's over. He's done.'

Later, I heard the board of trustees had been in a meeting together in early November and had decided to get rid of me. They claim they didn't, but I know they counted the votes to make sure they had the five votes necessary. Word around Columbus travels fast when it comes to OSU football, and it always got back to me very quickly.

The board had its five votes lined up, just waiting for something to happen. So we lost to Iowa, and I was fired on November 17. Losing three games in a row, getting fired, and then having to try and prepare to play Michigan. Imagine that, if you will. That's about as miserable as it gets.

This was a game no one ever thought we would win. I had been fired, and we'd spent the week in a fishbowl with all the sporting world watching. Bo and I gathered at midfield for our usual pregame chat. He talked about how nuts the people in Columbus were and what a treacherous place it was to coach football. Bo blasted the president of the University and the board of trustees. He said things I guess you would expect one coach to say to a fellow coach.

I remember the shock of the players' headbands. I always wanted one and only recently received one as a keepsake. I remember the great effort of the players—Chris Spielman, Tom Tupa, William White, Carlos Snow.

We began the game by sputtering, trying to find ourselves, and get the emotion out of the game. Jamie Morris gained 112 yards on fifteen carries in the first half. He annihilated us.

**WE WERE LOSING 13-0**, and yet we came back right before the end of the first half , and Tom Tupa throw a four-yard touchdown to Everett Ross, which made it 13-7, Michigan. But we were still in it.

I felt good about our chances in the locker room at halftime. I thought we showed we could come back. We got a slow start and had trouble making plays. I told the kids to work through it. I was very calm, and I told them what they had to do to win.

After halftime, our defense played great, and Tom Tupa threw a five-yard pass to Carlos Snow, who ran 70 yards for a touchdown and made the score 14-13. We scored again to make it 20-13, but missed the extra point. Michigan came back and tied it at 20.

On the possession leading up to Matt Franz's game-winning 26-yard field goal, Tom Tupa was literally knocked out of that ball game. Backup quarterback Greg Frey came in. I called a pass play. My coaches said I couldn't run that play because Frey wasn't ready.

'It's third down, for Chrissake,' I said. 'More than 10 and he's *gotta* throw the ball. We've got to keep possession. This is the Michigan game.'

Greg threw 18 yards to Vince Workman. Workman should have scored. Instead, he caught the ball for the first down and ran out of bounds. I'd like to have died! He could have cut up the field and run for days. Greg came out after one play, and Tupa came back in. But what a one play it was.

The big play on the final possession came when we had third and long. Michigan had a blitz on and we used Carlos Snow on a draw play. Michigan sent its corner man up the field and we ran right by everybody, while Michigan's running off with our receivers.

Snow went for about 30 yards, and with that three-point lead we kept it on the ground for the rest of the game. We finished on the Michigan two-yard line. We embarrassed them.

**MATT FRANZ'S FIELD GOAL WAS SO FITTING.** It helped him deal with missing that 41-yarder the year before. I was so proud of our football team. Shutting down Michigan and holding them to only seven second-half points was more than I could ever ask from these kids.

After the game was over and all the hoopla had died down, I walked across the stadium to say good-bye to Bo. 'I hate to lose,' he said, 'but today, I don't mind losing that game as much as I thought I would.'

I'm sure he said that out of friendship, but it was classy on his part. Bo was dejected at the loss, but he was secure in his position at Michigan. He could afford a loss to me that day.

When you look at the games, the wins and losses, it's hard to find another series of games in football decided by so few points either way. OSU vs. Michigan is a real tribute to the beauty of tradition.

I believe to this day that Woody would have survived the Gator Bowl incident had he not lost three years in a row to Michigan. There was no tolerance at Ohio State for losing THE GAME. Losing to Michigan was like committing a crime of treason. Coach Cooper can take solace with the fact that Ohio State has given him more chances than any previous coach ever dreamed of having.

Not many coaches were ever able to hold an edge over Bo Schembechler, so I'm pretty proud of my five win, four loss record against Michigan. There's never more pressure on any coach in college football than on an OSU coach before the Michigan game. And that hasn't changed. It was an unspoken creed.

And some things should never change.

# Art's dark side

We never knew Art Schlichter had a gambling problem. I knew Art went to the track when he was a student-athlete at Ohio State. I would see him there occasionally. He'd come over and talk to me, and I would sit with him and his parents if we were there at the same time.

⊃ *The good days: When gambling was essentially throwing on first down*

I knew from those casual conversations he had been to Las Vegas with his parents. His presence at the track and interest in horse racing didn't seem unusual, based on his roots. Art grew up in Washington Courthouse, Ohio, in a county known for its standardbred breeding and racing. I knew he gambled at the track, but I had no idea he had a gambling problem until after his days at Ohio State.

He came to me following his senior year at Ohio State, during his pro football career. He came to ask where he could borrow $200,000. My initial reaction was, 'You've got to be kidding me. I don't know anybody who has that kind of money to loan to someone.'

He told me his Dad needed it for the farm to help repay a loan. I asked him if he had considered John Galbraith. He said he already talked with the Galbraith family, but they wanted too much collateral. So I referred him to a friend who I felt might be able to at least point him in the direction of people with some money to help his father.

Not too long after Art's visit, my friend called and said, 'Earle, do you know what Art wanted?'

'Yeah,' I said, 'he wanted money to help save his family's farm.'

'Bullshit!' my buddy said. 'He didn't want money for the farm. I sent him out of here. He told me he's in gambling trouble and needs $200,000.'

'Gambling!' I said. 'What gambling? Betting what?'

My buddy said Art disclosed he was betting on basketball games but he didn't mention betting football games.

I started talking to some of his fellow Buckeye players. One told me me, 'Coach, you don't want to hear any of these stories about Art. They're pretty bad.'

Bit by bit, I was starting to learn about the other side of Art. Some of his activity did take place when he was a player, but it was without my knowledge and most certainly without my condonation. As the talk grew, so did the eagerness of some folks in Columbus to pin Art's problems on me.

I remember in particular Bob Hunter, a reporter from the *Columbus Dispatch*, asking me repeatedly, 'Did you take Art Schlichter to the track?'

I was always able to look him right in the eye and say no. Here's why. Art was a very private person. He was very much a loner. He would never have gone to the track with me. If he would have asked, I probably would have taken him. But he wouldn't have asked. He never wanted to be tied down. He always had to be in control. He went his own way.

**HE WASN'T A TEAM GUY.** He wasn't particularly close with his teammates. When he was a rising sophomore, we had a social gathering at my house and the captains chose the teams for the spring game. They made choice after choice, and they still hadn't picked Art. I was beginning to get upset with them. He would have been my *first* pick. I heard some of the guys whispering, 'Don't you take *him*.' I realized they were talking about Art. Finally, they took him—number seventeen. I was really surprised at that.

He was great with young people and old people. But he was uncomfortable with people in his own age bracket.

But I never thought Art had a problem. I go to the track and don't have a control problem. I can bet and walk away. I'd never put my family's financial well-being in jeopardy. I simply like horse racing. I've been to all the big races because I enjoy it. Some people don't believe in wagering. I look those people in the eye and say, 'Hey, don't you play the stock market? What the hell's the bigger gamble, me playing the horses or you playing the stock market?' Or how about the lottery?

The *Columbus Dispatch* really wanted to bury Earle Bruce because of Art Schlichter's trips to the track. The *Dispatch* tried to attack my integrity as a person by linking me to Art's downfall but without any factual basis.

The *Cleveland Plain Dealer* wrote an article about me and Art Schlichter, working the angle that I was involved in his problem. I called the *Plain Dealer* and said, 'What do you know about addiction?'

The reporter said he didn't know anything about addiction. 'You'd better learn about something before you write about it,' I told him.

Even Governor Celeste got in on the Earle Bruce witch-hunt. He was quoted in an Iowa paper as saying one of the reasons I was fired from Ohio State was for taking Art Schlichter to the track. That's when the Governor of Iowa responded by saying, 'If you don't want him, we'll take him.'

Art Schlichter was addicted, and he couldn't help himself. As a result, he did things he shouldn't have done, and he wound up in prison. I've visited him in the Ashland Correctional Facility in Ashland, Kentucky. I'd go again because I like Art.

HE WASN'T A BAD KID. He's someone with a very serious problem. Art Schlichter playing football—run and pass—with no distractions, was something to behold. But the outside influences working on Art Schlichter were too great.

When he was a student, he was supposed to live in a dorm, but he was living in a condo in Upper Arlington. I tried to put my foot down, but I finally decided it wasn't worth the problems. In retrospect, that was a huge mistake. I should have hammered him. Instead, I tolerated a lot of things I shouldn't have.

When he was a senior, I was named coach of the East-West Shrine game, and I selected Art as one of the quarterbacks. I told him he'd play the first and third quarter. But when the game was on the line in the fourth quarter, Art was begging me to play. He was so obnoxious on the sideline, I finally put him in. Even the network television camera man noticed it and said to me, "What kind of a baby is Schlichter anyway?"

Art was a high profile player but he should have been kicked in the ass about fourteen times. And I should have been the one to do it. But I didn't want to cause any problems with his family. Coming down hard on Art would have affected recruiting and caused all kinds of problems for our program. Instead, I tried to talk to him about his behavior. Whenever he was talking to me, I noticed he was biting his tongue.

'What are you *doing*?' I asked him.

'I got this nervous habit,' he said.

I now have a much better idea of all the things he had to be nervous about.


**ONE TIME I MET WITH ART** after the director of public relations at Scioto Downs, Chuck Stokes, called me and said Art was using their office phones. Chuck was afraid it might be to call in gambling bets. Chuck told me the guys Art associated with were involved in off-track betting, and he feared Art was taking part as well. When I sat down with Art to talk about my conversation with Chuck Stokes, he assured me they had it all wrong. Art explained he was just trying to call home.

Another time, a deputy sheriff told me Art went to a Touchdown Club hospitality suite and was seen rolling the dice and taking part in some card game. When I confronted Art, he vigorously denied being involved in the game. By coincidence, I had hired Art's old high school coach, Fred Zeckman, and called him in to get his take on everything I'd been hearing.

'Where there's smoke, there's FIRE,' I said. Zeckman said he didn't think Schlichter was doing anything wrong. Was he naïve? I guess we were *both* naïve. We didn't want to think Art was doing all that kind of stuff.

Art had exhibited some odd behavior that, at the time, I did not connect to gambling. After practice, he would spend a lot of time on the telephone. We'd wonder why he was always rushing to the phone. We figured he had a girlfriend, or that he had to talk to someone in his family.

Addicts are the greatest liars in the world. They can look you right in the eye and deny everything. Art did just that every time we confronted him with something we heard. He would earnestly proclaim, 'Coach, I wasn't gambling.'

As a coach I always tried to treat my players like my own kids. If my kids told me something, I tried to believe them until I was proven wrong. I treated Art the same way. So I had no idea Art's addiction had reached the critical stage that it really was.

I did discuss with Fred Zeckman again how suspect the whole situation felt. I remember telling him, 'What is all this smoke? Don't you think there has to be something to all this because of all this smoke? How could all of this talk have absolutely no substance?'

Later, I found out a local restaurateur loaned Art $35,000 and was never repaid. After his career at Ohio State, I found out about a lot of local business people who were hooked by Art for $100,000 or more. That piece of the story was never published in the *Dispatch* although they knew the names—just as I did.

**ART NEVER FINISHED AT OHIO STATE.** Basically, he dropped out to attend some of the All-Star games. Because he received automatic failures instead of incompletes, he could not return to Ohio State and pick up where he left off and get his degree. That's wrong. Let the punishment fit the crime. We need to do everything we can to keep the door open for athletes to return to school and earn their degrees. Giving them 'automatic failures' closes the door on them coming back and picking up their educations. The University could waive that rule and help out the athletes who have helped out the University.

I like Art Schlichter. He and I were always okay. I could sit down and talk with Art forever. I respect him and what he did on the football field. He was a good football player and a tough competitor. He never stayed down. He loved to practice. He played hurt. Off the football field, he had a lot of serious problems. He didn't always associate with the right people. And he didn't always get the best advice. I only hope that someday, Art will be able to claim his life back.

# Fired

When I was a little kid I heard
President Franklin Delano Roosevelt declare
December 7, 1941, as a day of infamy. That was the
day the Japanese attacked Pearl Harbor. For Earle
Bruce, the day of infamy was November 16, 1987.
That Monday afternoon, Athletic Director Rick Bay

*➲Sharing the sidelines: Bruce and Jennings in a more pastoral moment*

walked into my office and said 'Earle, it's over.

The president has decided to fire you and I have

resigned in protest.' The impact of his words were

somewhat similar to being kicked in the stomach

by a mule.

---

I had known something was up. After losing three games in a row—to Michigan State 13-7, Wisconsin 26-24, and Iowa 29-27, there were a lot of rumblings and I heard all of them. I got some telephone calls Sunday telling me everything was all right and I was going to come through this okay.

Friends were calling me to check in. Some of them were putting feelers out with folks in other circles to test the sentiment in town. Although they didn't want to tell me, they said the word on the street was I would be fired. Everybody had heard the talk. Both the trustees and the president were talking openly about their intentions while walking out of their booth after the Iowa loss.

One female board of trustee member, as she left the box, announced, 'It's over. It's over, he's done.' I got word on that immediately. You can't criticize the football coach in Columbus, Ohio, without it getting back to him quickly.

That Monday in November began normally with our early morning staff meeting. We ran through the meeting agenda, discussed the mistakes of the Iowa game, outlined our plans for Michigan, and talked about plans for practice that day. Regardless of what happened to me, the emphasis would still be on Michigan. I was fairly sure I was out—although nothing official had come down. My staff sensed it as well.

We had said before the Iowa game that losing that game could have dire effects. I knew the talk had to have some factual basis. Although I didn't specifically address my suspicions, every staff person in the room felt something big was looming.

As the meeting went on, the interruptions increased. I received several calls from my lawyer, John Zonak, and my wife. It became evident that the usual Monday media lunch at the Jai Lai would be a spectacle. Rumors were flying and every reporter in town wanted to get a piece of the big story—assuming there was one.

They would be asking questions about my job status, not about the upcoming game. John decided he would attend the lunch with me and we'd prepare a statement just in case. He also thought Jean should go as well. She never attended luncheons, but her presence was needed that day. We wanted to show that we were invested in the community and ready to fight to keep my job.

**WE WENT TO THE LUNCHEON.** The questions flew. I could tell from the nature of the questions that some pretty definite information about my fate had been shared. I'm sure some of those reporters knew more about the inside story than I ever would.

After the luncheon, I returned to my office in preparation for our scheduled team meeting at 2:15. About that time, Rick Bay walked in told me it was all over. I had been fired and he had resigned.

I remember telling Rick how I hated the idea that he was resigning. 'I can't be part of this,' he said. 'I have to leave. This is a travesty. This shouldn't be happening here.'

I didn't want him to leave his job as athletic director. He loved being at Ohio State and was doing a great job. He showed a lot of integrity in resigning, and I hated to see this happen to him.

You have to believe that the toughest time of anyone's life is after being fired. In fifteen minutes, Rick Bay had come and gone, and my days at Ohio State now had a finite number. I made only one call. I had to let Jean know we'd been fired. Even though I was in shock on some level, my mind had to get focused on Michigan, starting with that team meeting.

We had a schedule, and I had a whole room full of players waiting for me. What a performance I needed to give. The only thing that saved me was the fact I had been a football player. My coaches had taught me that if you get knocked down, you get up. Even if you're hurt, it doesn't mean it's over. I knew I had to pick myself up and start to fight again.

First, I met with the coaches for a brief time. I had to get to the players and tell them myself before the news leaked out. When I entered the meeting room, their faces looked blank. I told the team immediately I had been fired. Saturday would be my last game. I told them I would get them ready to play the game of their lives.

'Your character and mental toughness as a team is going to be under a microscope because we have lost three in a row,' I said. 'Everyone is going to be watching us because of what happened today. How you play is important to me because I recruited you and brought you here. I love you. I want you to hold nothing back this week. We are going to Ann Arbor and play the game of our lives. We will show everyone what this team is made of.'

I tried to gauge the response, but their faces were empty. There were lots of questions in their eyes, and I knew they were wondering not only about me but they were trying to figure out what this would do to the team and themselves personally. The seniors were particularly worried. I knew they would need lots of reassurance. The air had been knocked out of them, too.

**FROM THAT POINT ON**, we were focused on Michigan. Practice that Monday afternoon was weird. Everyone was going through the motions, and afterward, hundreds of people had gathered at the facility. I hated being stared at. Although most of the folks were for Earle Bruce there were those in attendance who were glad I'd been dumped.

I put on my game face, but inside I had an aching gut. Bill Myles arranged for a police escort so I could get to my car. I knew eating with the kids at training table would just be too much. I instructed my assistants to be with the team. I just wanted to get home.

I needed to get home and talk to my family. They were the ones who were affected the most. We have a very close family. We had always stuck together when there was a problem. I wanted to let them know we would fight through this together. What I wasn't aware of was the fact my whole family had already rallied. I had no idea about the drama underway at home.

It was like a funeral wake was in process. Jean's sister appeared from Findlay, although Jean hadn't even called her yet. The phone kept ringing. Wives of assistant coaches appeared at the door. Jean called the high school of my daughter, Aimee, to request her early dismissal so she could break the news to her in person. Jean called my daughter, Michele, at work to let her know. My oldest daughter, Lynn, had flown home immediately from a trip to Boston when she heard. Our youngest, Noel, was in the seventh grade and was walking home, unaware of anything unusual. Because of the crowd of people, she couldn't even get in the front door to go to the bathroom. And the phone kept ringing.

When I arrived home, my girls were all crying. I sat and talked to them. I told them that this was a setback, but we'd get through and be all right. How could I make them understand I was fired for reasons that had nothing to do with coaching?

IN THIS TYPE OF CRISIS, HOURS FLY BY. The phone kept ringing, and Bo was among the first to call me on my private line. Anne Hayes called to offer support. One of the most emotional and unforgettable things happened on Monday night after the firing. After finally getting home, I laid down on the family room couch. I just needed a moment of something normal. Then I heard lots of noise, like a band. It *was* a band. It was *the* band. The entire OSU Marching Band was in the yard.

I realized the marching band was outside playing—for me. I was struggling to keep my composure, and I didn't want to go out there. My daughters gathered around and urged me to go. It was the first time my daughters had seen me cry.

'You have to go out there,' Jean said.

The scene was unbelievable. I broke down. The Ohio State Marching Band was at *my* house in Worthington Hills playing the fight song, which had been a theme song in my life. I'm a fairly emotional guy and my emotions run very strong. I was standing there that night on my front porch, and I was thinking: *This is the last time I will have anything to do with the band.*

I remember thinking what competition and effort they gave, how four people compete for each position in the band. How they took coaching! They yelled and swore at each other to do better. Their drills sounded more like a football practice than a band practice. For nine years I had been invited to speak to the band on the night members are selected. When you go over there, it is a deafening, happy night.

The band waits for you to speak to them, and when you walk in the door they begin to chant 'Rose Bowl.' I have never experienced so much pressure in all my life as those nights, because it's clear which bowl game they want to march in. That night is the frenzied height of it all. No group is better than the band. It's the perfect example of *esprit d'corps*.

I stood with all these thoughts in my head, appreciating them coming out to play at such an emotional time for me. There are probably not many band members who remember coming to my house that night, but I will remember it forever. Never have I been so honored as I was that night.

SEVERAL OF MY FRIENDS kept cooking up ideas on how to get back at the powers that let me go. Some said I shouldn't coach the game, and then none of the assistants would coach, either. How would the game get played without coaches? Who would coach the team? I told them I could never do that to the kids.

My emphasis during the whole week of the game was to downplay the firing and build up the game with Michigan, because I wanted to win so bad. I knew it would be an uphill battle. All the critics thought we would pack it in and get slaughtered by Michigan.

That was not my approach at all. I wanted to win, and I wanted the kids to win. As a team, we agreed that no one was to talk about the firing and everyone was to concentrate on beating Michigan. I don't know if we actually were able to block out the firing, but the intensity of the Michigan rivalry did wonders for our focus. It was a good feeling to just concentrate on the prize—the best victory you can have as an OSU coach—Michigan.

Each day of that week was more unreal than the next. I did begin to mentally acknowledge that the series of 'last times' had begun. There were protestors outside practice each afternoon. They were a vocal group of Bruce supporters. The media had painted me as a guy with no personality or friends. Yes, I had my detractors—but I also had plenty of backers, too.

They actually thought they could change the outcome of my firing. But they had no idea my dismissal had nothing to do with my performance as a coach. One of the television stations had conducted an informal call-in poll Monday night to measure the opinion on my firing. Callers replied to the question 'Should Earle Bruce have been fired?'

The results were 1,192—yes, 11,303—no. For a guy with no support, I seemed to have found a few friends somewhere along the line.

TUESDAY, WEDNESDAY, AND THURSDAY of that week are a blur. Michigan remained our priority. I do remember Tuesday being significant because it was the day we delivered our letter to President Jennings. My lawyer composed a letter to simply ask for an official explanation of why I had been fired and what the contract settlement would be. Up to that point, no one from the University besides Rick Bay had contacted me. I had no direction to work from. I had no confirmation that I was even supposed to coach the Michigan game.

⊃*Last rites: The players sprout "Earle" headbands for the Michigan game*

I had just planned to finish the season out for the benefit of the team. Wednesday was important because it marked another day without a word from the president's office. Finally, on Thursday, I heard from the president. No personal contact, only a letter. It gave no reason for the firing. It basically said the University was cutting me loose. I was gone without an explanation, not a dollar for the broken contract, or a thank you. Just a kick in the ass.

Up until that letter, I would have done anything to stay at OSU and fight to get my job back. The letter changed everything. Its cool, impersonal tone set me on fire. This was now war. Even Jean abandoned her usual calm and said, 'We're going to sue.'

We had the Senior Tackle immediately following Friday's practice. It was one of the most cherished traditions in the life of an Ohio State football player. Each senior hits the tackling dummy for one final time while teammates highlight that player's career. It's usually in the stadium and open to fans and has a pep rally feeling. That day it was more like a circus.

A plane had been flying around with a banner proclaiming 'Fire Jennings—not Bruce.' I was a little apprehensive how this would end and decided to move the senior tackle portion to the indoor facility. The seniors hit the sled, and the other players talked about them. The senior captains asked *me* to hit the sled since it would be my last time there. I hit the sled. The clock in my head began the countdown. We got ready to go to Michigan.

Jean sent a note with me for the players. I decided to read it to them after breakfast. It was Jean at her best—just saying how proud she and the other coaches' wives were of the team. She wrote how they'd always be near to her heart and how she would miss them. There was nothing I could say after that. I remember the coin toss after the pre-game warm-ups. We were ready to go out on field and the whole football team gathered to go out, not just the captain.

I thought 'Geez, this is really gonna be some game.' So we're all standing out there and the team is behind me. I turn to look at the team and they've all removed their helmets and they got something around their heads. I said, 'What the hell have they got on?'

I couldn't see what it said. I thought, 'What's going on? What's the matter with these guys—we don't do this kind of stuff.'

Then I saw they were all wearing headbands that said 'Earle.' It took me a second to get the idea this was a positive show of support. I tried to ignore it, but I had to ask the assistant coaches what was up. I was told that offensive lineman Joe Staysniak got the idea revved up and had everyone wear them in support of me.

No one wanted to tell me who started it, because they weren't sure how I'd take it. It was a tremendous gesture. But once the game started, I'd never had known it. Calling plays in the Michigan game was all I was focused on. I was doing everything possible to win that game. I thought a win was the best statement possible to prove to everyone there were no coaching problems at Ohio State. We had good kids who worked at practice and played hard in battle. That's the best sign that everything is running right.

If the game is a history maker, and it certainly was, we were off to a poor start. We got behind 13-0 pretty quick. We fought back to score before the half and made it 13-7. At half time I think they had settled down some. They had been highly emotional, and they were missing tackles and not connecting on some things, but they got over those jitters.

On the first series of the second half, we threw a little five-yard pass to Carlos Snow out in the flat, and he ran it 70 yards for a touchdown. We went ahead 14-13 and never looked back. When the game ended, we had won, 23-20, and we were down on the two-yard line when time ran out. We could have scored with a field goal if we had to, but we were trying to run out the clock. We fought to become the dominant factor in the second half, and we won that football game. It was not a gift. The kids were faced with a daunting set of circumstances and they never faltered. I knew they would take that lesson with them for the rest of their lives.

**THE MINUTES AFTER THE GAME WERE A BLUR.** There was so much going on simultaneously that my brain was on overdrive. I remember being on the players' shoulders, the fans were rushing the field, people were trying to grab my hat. Everything moved so fast. I was caught up in all the glory of that moment. There was no time to think. The firing took a back seat to this incredible accomplishment. I was emotionally drained but the realization that we had prevailed against all odds began to sink in. I was so proud of those kids and their refusal to give up.

When we assembled in the locker room, I didn't want the moment to end. I knew it would never be like this again. After this day, they would go their way and I would go mine—a destination for me that was totally unknown. I was overwhelmed with pride as I talked to the players.

When everybody was cleared out, I was the last one to leave the locker room. I decided to go see Bo. I was directed back to his locker room and there he was talking to a recruit, an Ohio kid, Kirk Herbstreit. I stood there for a second and looked at Kirk and said, 'Hey, what are you doing? You're not going to *Michigan*, you're going to Ohio State!'

Bo and I talked for awhile, about the game, about my situation. He said, 'I never want to lose. Never! But if we have to lose to Ohio State, this is a loss I can accept.' I remember thinking how much it took for him to say that.

I don't know how many of you have been fired from a job, but it is the strongest form of failure. The hurt keeps burning. I'd never been fired before, and naïvely, I thought I never would.

One of the awful side effects is the way it sifts out your friends. You collect a lot of friends in a lifetime. Some you are blessed to have because you can count on them any time at all. There is another category of friends who are fair-weather, and you have them when everything is going well. They might like you, but they can't handle being associated with you if you become unpopular. Even if they want to maintain a friendship with you, they cannot. They need to remain friends with those who can best benefit them.

When I look at that time, many were friendly to me, giving me all kinds of stories and reassurances before the firing. They said, 'Oh, it's not going to happen, Earle, it's not going to happen,' But when I was let go, I never saw them again. I'd always known I had friends in both categories. The firing just confirmed what I already knew in my gut. I still see those 'friends' around Columbus today, and I'll never forget what category they fell in.

I was a godsend for John Cooper. The way I was fired was so appalling that no one else would be fired that way again.

# Aftermath

The support for me throughout the community was overwhelming. We received hundreds of phone calls at home, which Jean handled. Given that it was Michigan week, I wasn't out in public very much. I didn't run into many people outside the football team and its

*⊃Fan-tastic: Well-wishers crowd way to locker room after Michigan win*

immediate family. My friend and personal attorney, John Zonak, convinced me to sue Jennings and the University. It doesn't do you any good to sue the school, and frankly, I didn't want to. But I felt I had to protect my family. What if I never received another job offer? What if this was it—at age 56? I had never been fired before. I didn't know what kind of brand it would leave on me for future positions.

Zonak and I had written a letter to the University asking how I was going to be treated, meaning what kind of termination package was being proposed. Instead of an explanation, we got a curt letter saying there wasn't going to be anything. No talk of honoring the remaining term of my contract. They apparently were just going to kick me out on my ass.

Their reply left me without with much choice. Jean actually made the decision. She loved Ohio State as much as I did. But she felt no one should be treated this way. 'Sue them,' she told me.

The actual lawsuit was filed the Friday before the Michigan game. It asked for a settlement of $7.4 million and was your basic 'breach of contract' lawsuit, saying Jennings was 'part of a scheme...and in bad faith made false and untrue statements' about me. Jennings' 'intentional, malicious...statements and implications also indicated that the plaintiff was too old for the position of head football coach.' Further, Jennings' actions caused, 'the plaintiff and his family to be outraged, subjected to humiliation, shame, anxiety, grief and rage and...severe mental and physical distress.'

Attached to the suit were requests for three depositions from three women. Jennings' wife, who he had just separated from after 28 years; Barbara Real, director of OSU's regional fund-raising campaigns; and Board of Trustee member Deborah Casto, who had been very outspoken in her dislike of me. We asked for depositions from Mrs. Jennings and Real that would provide financial records pertaining to Jennings.

No one knew we filed the lawsuit. Zonak did it very quietly late Friday when everyone had their attention on what was happening in Ann Arbor. I announced the lawsuit on my coach's show Saturday night after the Michigan game. All the assistant coaches gathered at my home in Worthington to watch the show. Jean and my girls told me everyone erupted into cheering and applause when I announced I was suing Jennings.

I named the University, but the problem all along was Jennings. If the guy is going to attack me and my family, then he needs to be more perfect than Jennings seemed to be. He would not tell me why I was being fired. I thought his motivation was because my firing would take the spotlight off *him*. The Cleveland paper was writing that he had been warned *his* job was in jeopardy, because of his personal life. The Cleveland reporters even found out Jennings and Real had plane tickets to fly to London together for a vacation.

**AFTER THAT WELL DOCUMENTED LITTLE EPISODE**, the tide seemed to change. Zonak was asked to sit down and talk. After several days of discussion, Zonak flew down to Florida where I had escaped to my condo. Zonak said he'd come with a settlement that was probably the best we could realistically get. I was to be paid $471,000. The money was broken down to include the years of salary left on my contract and fringe benefits. To this day, I'm a little bitter about the settlement. Jennings cost me $1,000 a month retirement by refusing to buy my five years retirement time. I had thirty years service with the state teacher's retirement system—just five short of a big bump in pension rates. Other athletic staff were permitted this buyout, even my recruiting coordinator. But Jennings tried to put it to me every way he could.

He never told me why he fired me. I always asked to be told and was finally granted an eight-minute meeting with him. 'I don't have to give a reason,' he said.

There are a lot of people within the coaching profession who knew what Jennings was. That was my only salvation. When they looked into why Earle Bruce was fired, they saw Earle Bruce wasn't fired because of his football record or because he was a no good son-of-a-bitch. I was fired because I pissed off the Columbus power structure, including members of the prominent Wolfe family, publishers of the local newspaper. All the political people in Columbus bow to the Wolfe family and I failed to do it. Not many in Columbus fight the Wolfe family, and Jennings was no exception.

**THE SEEDS OF MY FIRING** were planted back in 1982 and 1983 when I was forced to move my coach's show from Wolfe's WBNS-TV (Channel 10). A week before national signing day, Columbus' NBC affiliate (Channel 4) asked me to do an interview the night of national signing day. We agreed to do something within their 5:30 news. No problem. A couple of days later, Channel 6, the ABC affiliate, called and asked me to do something with them in the 6 o'clock news. I told then I would be meeting with our quarterbacks at that time, but we were able to work it out and I said that would be fine. Then, right before signing day, Channel 10 called. I told them I had a real problem because I had committed to the two other stations. They told me I'd have to move one of those since they had to be #1 because they did my TV show.

I told them they were #1 with me, but they should have called me sooner. The other two stations called me a week ahead of time. As it turned out, everyone brought their mobile units over and only Channel 10's worked. So Channel 10 (WBNS) got the interview.

The next morning, my phone rang and it was WBNS general manager, Gene D'Angelo, one of the most powerful men within the Wolfe organization.

'We're cutting the cord,' he said.

I asked him what he was talking about. He told me the way I handled that whole signing day interview thing was bullshit and they'd had it. In retrospect, I should have told him that I'd come down and we'd talk about it. But I just sort of blew him off, thinking it was a little hotheaded and he'd get over it. Well, he *didn't* get over it.

Everyone at Channel 10 had always treated me first class, but D'Angelo was a spur-of-the-moment kind of guy, and if he got pissed, it was all over. He once told me, 'You're either with us, or against us.' That seemed to be the trademark Wolfe philosophy. Columbus is owned by them, and they don't like to be challenged in Columbus, Ohio.

**I SHOULD HAVE SEEN THE SIGNS** from the day I started. My first day on the job, I was having lunch and saw an old physical education professor. We chatted at some length and I remember his advice to me: 'Don't let the people downtown own you.' He did some moonlighting as 'The Judge' on Channel 10 and told me, 'If you bring a television show here, let ALL the stations have a shot at it.'

Athletic Director Hugh Hindman told me he'd put my TV show out to bid, but he told me WBNS-TV would win because they'd bid the highest. The other two stations bid $12,000 and $14,000, but sure enough, WBNS-TV bid $36,000—matching my salary at Iowa State! It was a no-contest. By contrast, Woody only made $15,000 on his TV show. But I soon found out what my old friend meant by not letting the downtown people own you.

Zonak told me they put an awful lot of pressure on him after he filed that lawsuit. If you ever file a lawsuit against 'the establishment' in Columbus, Ohio, don't use a local lawyer. I loved John Zonak to death.

He was a dear friend and a wonderful man. But he got hell from all the prominent people in town for his outspoken comments about some of the elite members of the Columbus power structure. The pressure of being honest and outspoken is just too much for a local attorney.

You can say all you want about the Wolfe family, Channel 10, the *Dispatch*, and everything else. They all played a role. But the guy who was the most responsible for my firing was Jennings. Over the years, I've heard just about as many stories about Jennings as I have Woody Hayes. Only the Jennings stories aren't positive ones.

The great coach Pat Dye once worked for Jennings at Wyoming. Pat had a job interview at Auburn. Before leaving for the interview, Dye had a discussion with Jennings. Pat recalls that Jennings said, 'If you go, you don't have a job.' Imagine that. Coach Dye actually resigned before he left for the interview.

Jennings fired everybody. He fired seven vice-presidents, the athletic director, helped fire basketball coach Eldon Miller, and I was the next on his list. I even told Rick Bay when he was hired, his main job would be to fire us. I despised that Jennings wanted to close the University airport and the popular University golf course. He closed the main entrance to the University, off High Street, something a real Buckeye would never have considered doing. To walk in through that gorgeous, historic entrance with a sea of beautiful green landscape was something. The famous campus oval and library stretched out in front of you. What a sight! I saw that sight daily as a student and for years as a coach. Jennings wasn't able to love anything but his reflection in the mirror.

**I WAS A BUCKEYE FROM THE FIRST TIME** I saw the band come onto the field before the Missouri football game in 1949. The drum major threw that baton into the air and the hair on the back of my neck stood up. I've been a Buckeye through and through ever since that moment.

To this day, I have a recurring dream about that man. I outlined this dream in a rough manuscript of this book. I wanted everyone to know how I feel about Jennings and what he did to me and my University. Unfortunately, my dream didn't make the final edit—the legal review. I can't figure out the harm—it's only a harmless dream, for God's sake. Although I gotta tell you, when I have this dream, it seems damn real and damn fitting. My subconscious is the only place where the pain Jennings caused me, my family, and those who loved OSU football is reconciled. And the best part of the dream is the morning after. I wake up good and refreshed.

He was an embarrassment and a disgrace to that proud and distinguished University. *My* University. He hated me because of my image—because I wouldn't hide in a slick suit. Because I wouldn't kiss the asses of the right folks. Because I was first and foremost a football coach.

I thought that was my job. I kept all my evaluation slips. My evaluations were always above average. Even the Associated Press ran a story after my firing that outlined my final evaluation, which had come seven months before my firing. I scored eight or above on a ten-point scale in every category. I was 81-26-1 at OSU, best in the Big Ten during my nine years, and I had a winning record against Michigan.

A University president has the right to fire anyone for just cause. But the firing should be straight-forward, above-board. The shame of it was this: I was the most loyal Ohio Stater ever, and I was treated like the worst of outlaws. I had worked terribly hard to become the coach of Ohio State, I was good at it, and Jennings took my coaching life from me.

# Moving on

After my demise at Ohio

State, I was blessed with several opportunities to coach.

First, I was considered for an opening at Kansas.

I turned down the job, and that, in retrospect, was

probably a mistake. Kansas wanted to re-establish

their program, and that had become my strength

*⊃On the road again: the tools of the coaching trade always seem to include a roadmap*

through the years, taking a program that had been

on a down slide and injecting it with some new

life. But my friends and colleagues whose advice

I trusted told me to sit out for a year and let the dust

settle. So, reluctantly, I turned down Kansas

and stayed out of college coaching for awhile.

———————————————————————

In June, I noticed in the newspaper an opening for football coach at Northern Iowa. If it had been anywhere other than Iowa, I probably wouldn't have been interested. But having coached in Iowa previously, I loved the people there. I knew that I could go to Northern Iowa and be happy. Eldon Miller went to Northern Iowa after Jennings fired him as basketball coach at Ohio State. I talked with Eldon by phone, and he asked if I knew of any assistant or up-and-coming head coach who would be interested in the job at Northern Iowa. I told him I'd think about likely candidates and call him back a couple of days later.

When I called him back, I said, 'Yeah, I *do* know a guy who's interested—ME.'

So with Eldon's help, an interview was arranged, they offered me the job, and I accepted it. As we're driving back to Columbus, I look at Jean, and she is crying. She didn't want to leave Columbus. She didn't want our youngest daughter, Noel, to leave school and move to Iowa. I felt bad to see someone as tough as my wife cry.

But I felt strongly about the opportunity. 'I've got to do this,' I told her. 'I want to do this. I *want* to be a head coach.'

In my five-year contract with Northern Iowa, I stipulated that I could leave if I received an offer from any of five schools I identified. We opened the season against Pittsburgh. We played Iowa State off their feet and lost at the last minute. We had some great coaches already on staff and added to the talent with other great coaches who came with me from Ohio State.

I was able to get Tom Lichtenberg to move to Iowa from Ohio. Steve Szabo, who I had to fire at Ohio State, I hired at Northern Iowa. Northern Iowa had a winning program, but Division One Double-A was a little different league. One of the biggest challenges was the granting of partial scholarships. Double-A schools would break down some of their full scholarships, and apportion it out to, say, two players. I had never worked this way, and I wasn't comfortable with it. If you're recruiting a great talent, it's hard to compete with the likes of Iowa State or Iowa, who could offer a full ride. I hadn't had any experience at that level.

Darryl Mudra and most of the assistants were good at compensating for the lack of full scholarships, but I wasn't. Financially, the school was going through a crisis. We needed a lot of fund-raising. Finally, one day, I talked with Athletic Director Bob Bowlsby, about the frustrations of recruiting.

He looked at me and said, 'Well, if it's that costly maybe we ought to drop football.'

What! You don't say 'drop football' to me! He's talking about dropping football and I'm here? So I starting thinking about getting out of there while the getting was good.

ONE OF MY LONG-TIME FRIENDS, Oval Jaynes, the athletic director at Colorado State, called and asked if I'd be interested in coming out to Colorado State. I was. It was tough to leave Northern Iowa, and I had to pay $100,000 to get out of my contract because Colorado State wasn't one of the five schools I had specified in my contract.

It took all the money I got from my house in Columbus to get out of the Northern Iowa contract. When I resigned at Northern Iowa, Bowlsby gave me a list of ten other things I had to pay for. He said expenses had been incurred only because I was the coach. I had to pay $30,000 for a charter airplane that took our team to Southern Illinois. I had to personally pay for a new blocking sled the team used for conditioning. Bowlsby maintained he wouldn't have purchased it if I hadn't been the coach.

The list went on and on. Northern Iowa wanted $140,000 but settled for $100,000. So we settled at Northern Iowa and I was off to pursue an opening out west.

Colorado State had fired their coach, who had been there ten years. I went out to CSU before Christmas in 1988 for an interview. Colorado State's president looked me right in the eye and said, 'We want you to be our football coach. We want you to come in here and build our football program and give us some discipline.'

I said, 'You're gonna get discipline. And you'll get a rebuilt program.'

'That's what we want,' he said.

Discipline was never a problem for me. When I went to Colorado State, even the players told me the team needed discipline.

'Don't worry about that,' I told them. 'You'll get discipline like you've never had it before.'

My first year, about ten football players got in a big fight during the winter. I get all the names of the football players and, one by one, I call them into my office.

'Hey,' I said. 'I heard you've been fighting. Now starting tomorrow at 6 a.m., we're gonna meet out at the stadium and you're gonna run.'

The snow was about five inches deep when I got there the next morning, but the kids were there. The ability to install a disciplined regime was why I was hired.

**IN 1990, I TOOK THE COLORADO STATE** team to the Freedom Bowl. My first team quarterback and fullback roomed together in the team hotel. One morning at 3 a.m. I got a call from the hotel security.

'We got a problem,' he said. 'They delivered a pizza to room 204, and your players won't pay the pizza man.'

I was so pissed I told those two players I was sending them home. Then I started thinking about all the bad publicity we'd get and how the team didn't deserve it. So I called those guys back at 5:30 a.m. and said, 'You get your asses down here before anybody else gets up. I'm going to take you back on the football team, and the only people who will know about this are the people you tell. But you're grounded the rest of the trip and you're up every morning at 5:30 running.'

I got the offensive backfield coach in a car and those two players running right behind us. I drove, and I drove. Finally my assistant said, 'Coach, how far are you going to go?'

'Until they drop,' I told him.

This routine continued until the morning of the game. Scheduled as a night game, my backfield coach wondered if I'd run 'em.

'You're goddamn right we're gonna run 'em. What do you mean?'

'Well,' he says, 'it's Game Day.'

'I don't give a shit,' I said. 'They deserve to run, they don't even deserve to play.'

So I ran them both and neither one started the game that night. But when I did put them in, the fullback ran a touchdown for 55 yards. He'd never run 55 yards in his life. And the quarterback, who didn't start the game, had two long touchdown passes, which clinched the win, 32-31.

One of those players, Mike Gimenez, is coaching his hometown high school now. I was honored when he asked me to come and speak to his team. Discipline was simply a set of rules to live by. It wasn't personal.

**THE CSU PRESIDENT** was a tremendous person. I could look him right in the eye and tell he was going to be a man of his word. Unfortunately, he went to Alabama a year and a half later. It was a great four-year stint at Colorado State. Our first year record in 1989 was 5-5-1. We were 9-4 the next year and won the Freedom Bowl over Oregon by one point.

In 1991, we were 3 and 8, losing to Air Force, Nebraska, Southern Mississippi, Utah, Wyoming, BYU, San Diego State, and New Mexico State. Our team scored a lot of points, but we couldn't win.

That year, I recruited the best players ever at Colorado State, and we did better the next year. But the administration totally changed at CSU. The president left for Alabama and the athletic director went to Pittsburgh. Here I was with a new president and a new athletic director again. I didn't like the feeling.

When Oval Jaynes resigned to go to Pittsburgh, the new president at Colorado State called me and promised me a say in who was going to be the new athletic director. Some folks advised me to go for the athletic director's job myself, but I didn't, which was probably a mistake.

Outside candidates included a former OSU assistant, Dan Meinhert, who came in for an interview. Long Beach State Athletic Director Cory Johnson, considered an 'up and comer' among athletic directors, was being interviewed. There were also candidates from inside the school.

During the process, I had lunch with all four candidates, and the last guy I had lunch with was Cory Johnson. Something about our conversation struck me, and while we were eating, I leaned over to him and said, 'You already have the job here, don't you?'

He didn't say yes or no, but I told him I could tell in his demeanor that he knew he had the job. He came across a lot more arrogant than I might have expected, which perturbed me a bit. After lunch, I returned to the office and saw the assistant athletic director in the parking lot. He was a candidate, too, and had just been told someone else had been hired. I checked with our basketball coach, and he told me he didn't have any input either.

**So we went to Nebraska to play football.** Sunday morning when I got back, the president called me and asked me to rank the contenders. I told him my first choice was the guy from Kentucky, my second choice was the Minnesota candidate, and my third pick was our guy from the staff.

I said the guy I really didn't want to work with was Cory Johnson.

The president set me up. I could tell during my lunch with Cory Johnson he had already been promised the job. I told him he was getting the job. This, after the president promised I would have some input. We talked a few more minutes, and he said, 'Can you work with Cory Johnson?'

'Is he the new athletic director?' I asked.

'I've hired Cory Johnson as the athletic director,' he said.

'I guess I can work with anybody,' I said.

After being promised input and given bullshit, you can imagine what I thought of the president.

I thought Cory Johnson was a snake. It didn't take long for him to start making what I thought were some terrible decisions that hurt the athletic department. The last game of the 1992 season was at New Mexico. The night before the game, a reporter with one of the local papers came up to me and said, 'Earle, you're going to be fired Sunday after the game.'

I looked at her in utter amazement and said, 'What are you talking about?' I was dumbfounded. There's no way they could fire me. I hadn't done anything wrong. We were on the right track.

After the game, I called some friends of mine in some fairly high places, including one of the owners of the Rockies franchise, and he confirmed that, indeed, my head was on the block.

**I WAS BEING ACCUSED OF RACISM**, violating NCAA rules, and abusing players. No one had ever accused me of anything like that in my life. I called the CSU president Saturday night when we returned from Nebraska, and I asked if I could come over to his house.

He confirmed much of what I had learned. We had a third-string quarterback—a kid I really loved—a great kid and a straight A student and he said he thought he was being abused on the football field. Now Colorado is a pretty liberal place, and football is a tough game. The old traditional in-your-face style of coaching had clashed with the more liberal hands-off, let-everybody-do-his-own-thing' attitude.

If an athletic director changes, or a school superintendent, you are always subject to being fired. I was too naïve to ever realize that. They accused me of assaulting the kids on my own team at Colorado State. 'Hey,' I asked some of my former players, 'how many times did I grab your facemask and shake you around a little?' Most of them said they thought that was part of the territory.

None of my first-team players were involved in that allegation at CSU. It was a third-team quarterback and a third-team tight end. My first- and second-team players tried to get members of the administration to talk to them about the allegations, but no one paid much attention to what these kids were saying. They were taking the word of a couple of malcontents who didn't even play.

The president of the university didn't understand football and its toughness. The man who hired me said he wanted toughness and discipline. But when he left, the rules changed. And I didn't get that. I was still being a football coach.

**THERE WAS A SENSE ON MY PART** that the decision was made by Cory Johnson and backed by the president and there wasn't a lot I could do about it. Ultimately, the school announced my firing. I held my own news conference to tell my side of the story. I was doing OK until I saw about fifteen of my players come to the news conference, and I broke down a little bit.

I really loved my kids at Colorado State. And to see my kids sitting in front of me in support was very reassuring. Those kids knew I was being set up and they felt badly for me and for the CSU program, but there wasn't anything any of us could do. That was the part of the news conference that was used everywhere from Colorado to Columbus, of course. I tried to ask in my news conference how Cory Johnson and the president could do this. In all my coaching, I never hurt anyone. Sure, it got physical. Sure, I'd grab a player by the facemask, or shove and punch at his pads to make a point. That's the way it was.

For Cory Johnson to make his point, he recruited about fifteen of my second- and third-stringers—kids who didn't play much—to come in and sing a story about how they were being abused. What a tactic.

It was obvious to me that Cory Johnson wanted his own man. I learned after it was all over, that for some time he had been talking with Sonny Lubeck, a friend of his, about coming to succeed me at CSU.

I invited President Yates and his chief counsel to the training table to talk with the players. I'm not the best person in the world with names, so appreciate it when I tell you that I introduced the man who just fired me, President Al Yates, to my team as 'President *Ed* Yates.'

Four or five of the players started to laugh, and later they came up to me and said, 'You're in trouble. You called him *Ed* instead of *Al*.'

Oh my God, I thought.

I wrote him a note and apologized and made sure that I called him Al Yates in the letter. It was the second time I had called him Ed. Once, speaking to his wife at their private country club, I called him Ed. I guess I've met more Ed Yateses than Al Yateses.

After my firing, my starting fullback said, 'You're being fired because you called him Ed.'

He was probably right.


**WE RECRUITED SOME GREAT FOOTBALL PLAYERS** at Colorado State and some of them advanced to the pro ranks. Getting players to come to Colorado State was tough. The facilities were limited and unimpressive. There was very little tradition. Our football coaching staff did an admirable job of bringing in good players.

My proudest moment at Colorado State came in winning the Freedom Bowl in 1990, the first bowl game ever won at CSU. We were a story. We hadn't been to a bowl game in forty years and our kids wanted to go. After the season, we were picked to go to the Freedom Bowl, we were 17-point underdogs to Oregon, and we came from behind to win by one point.

My CSU settlement provided my salary for a year. I had a two-year contract remaining, and I would be paid for a year. I was going to stay in Colorado, but Cory Johnson lived down the street from me. After all the terrible things he said about me, I told Jean, 'We have to get out of here. I can't stand being on the same street with the man who purposely chose to ruin my life here in Colorado.'

My sister and brother-in-law were relocating to Wilmington, North Carolina, and Jean and I decided to move there as well. We moved to Wilmington in August of 1993. On a trip to Columbus to visit my kids, some of my friends suggested I talk with my old friend, Perry Frey, at WTVN Radio about doing on-air work during the Ohio State football season.

Perry said he couldn't pay me very much to start out. I said that was all right. Everyone thought I'd be real critical of Ohio State. But those people didn't know Earle Bruce. I was still a Buckeye. I may not like some of the things I see, but I always want the best for the program.

The newspaper set me up and roasted me pretty good one time about comments I made about Andy Katzenmoyer not playing up to his potential. All the coaches said they thought he was playing well. What do you expect the coaches to say? Ohio State has always had a pretty good mouthpiece in the *Dispatch,* so they took out after me, too. I was hoping to help the kid and fire him up to play better.

The paper wanted to make me the negative guy, so they used me. I'm sure there were some hard feelings. I love to go to practice and watch game film with the coaches. But after the Katzenmoyer article in the paper, I didn't think I could go.

**RADIO HAS BEEN FUN.** It's given the fans a chance to get to know more of Earle Bruce, and it's given Earle Bruce a chance to get to know more about the fans. The fans have treated me exceptionally. They always have. The media portrayed me as without passion, and difficult to know. Now that I've done some writing and recording, everyone knows how I really am.

Coach Cooper and his staff have always welcomed me. I knew all about John Cooper before he came to Ohio State. He played at Iowa State, and he was a great player on the dirty/thirty football team. Iowa State's football team at that time was known for its aggressive play. Only the toughest survived camp and practice, and only thirty kids played. John was a tough football player who ran to hit you. He might not have been the fastest thing in the world, but he ran to hit you.

When I started at WTVN, you could almost see the pressure building on John Cooper. Now he seems more relaxed. His approach to people is much better than when he was under the gun. He's done a great job of winning and turning things around. He's involved in the coaching more than what I saw when I first came here. He seems more positive and confident about his job than he used to be.

He's always been very good to me, and I've always appreciated the way he's treated me. I've always been made to feel welcome. I've talked with the team, even spoke at the senior tackle before the Michigan game. Unfortunately, Lloyd Carr and the Michigan team watched senior tackle from their hotel rooms and some of the stuff I said fired Michigan's players up more than it fired up the Ohio State players.

Still, I showed up in my suit and fedora, and about 45,000 fans turned out to watch. We got some scarlet and gray blood boiling. It was one of the biggest honors I could have. I remember being a little in awe because I had never seen a senior tackle that well-attended. That wasn't what senior tackle was originally designed to be. Now it's scaled back to what it was really intended to be—a small get-together with the team and family members to honor the seniors with one final hit of the blocking sled.

BEING ASSOCIATED with WTVN Radio has allowed me to stay close to the football program and the game. I enjoy talking to the fans and coaches about the game. I enjoy the programming we do. I've learned some things from the professional broadcasters, and I've come to appreciate the planning and timing involved in making a broadcast work. A lot of our success has to do with the chemistry of our on-air team. Our group has included several Buckeyes—Greg Frey, Jim Lachey, Chris Spielman, Dave Purdy and Bobby Hoying.

We take exception to what each other says once in a while, and that adds to the excitement of the shows. We've had a lot of fun on the road. We hit all the top steakhouses, and we enjoy each other's company. Once, we had to drive all night to get home from Chicago when we missed our flight from Midway. After the 1999 Sugar Bowl, we drove home from New Orleans when our flights were cancelled because of the weather and we had no place to stay, no way to get home, and no word on when we'd be able to fly out of New Orleans. We drove straight through, into the Midwest snow storm, and arrived home about sixteen hours later.

Another time, Greg Frey took a wrong turn as we were leaving the University of Washington Stadium. We drove around two huge lakes in the Seattle area for about an hour trying to get back to where we started. I don't let him forget about that. When we drive to games, it's always a quick trip to our destination. But coming home, it seems we have to stop at every restroom along the interstate. And it's been an ongoing struggle for WTVN to work with Ohio State. Ohio State officials have even gone out of their way to keep us from broadcasting at away game sites. And they won't let us wear any WTVN clothing with the OSU logo on it. I've really been made aware of the business side of college football and how far away from the football field it really extends.

**I MAY NOT BREATHE** into the microphone the right way. I may not talk right. I may not be the most professional broadcaster you've ever heard. But I give it to you straight from the heart. I'm not phoney. I tell it to you the way it is. I've always been that way.

A lot of people say I didn't have a personality. Now they act amazed to hear me on the radio. Members of the Boosters Club and the Quarterback Club knew there was another dimension to me. I can kid and joke once in awhile. I'm not a stuffed shirt. But that's the way I was portrayed for many years in Columbus.

I'm still a football coach at heart. If I have any free time, my mind wanders to football, and I'm in a reverie. Sometimes I watch the old college games on one of the history channels—Notre Dame, Michigan, Ohio State, all in black and white. I analyze, I look for tendencies. I break film down. I am *coaching*.

I loved that life. Building a team, running a play to perfection, lifting the players above themselves. My life has been damn good. It's worked out great.

# Index

George Lehner is employed as Sports Director at WTVN Radio
in Columbus, Ohio. He has won numerous awards for his coverage
of Ohio State football. A native of Massillon, Ohio, George has followed
the career of Coach Earle Bruce since he coached Massillon to two
straight undefeated seasons in the 1960s. George and Earle also work
together on WTVN's coverage of Ohio State football.

Darcy Lehner is a graduate of the Ohio University School of Journalism.
She has worked in the marketing and public relations field for twenty
years, specializing in the areas of retirement housing and association
marketing. She has written for several trade magazines and community
papers including, American Health Care Association's *Provider* magazine,
*WOSU AirFare* and *Columbus Alive*.

The Lehners live in Gahanna, Ohio, with their three children.